what TO write

TO MAKE MEANINGFUL ALBUMS

by Melody Ross

Published by Chatterbox, LLC

Photography and Graphic Design by Kelly Frew
Project coordinator– Christy Tomlinson

The use of products and trademark names are for information purposes only, with no intention of infringement
upon those trademarks.

For information about bulk sales or promotional pricing,
please contact Customer Service at
info@chatterboxinc.com.

1.888.416.6260

2141 W. Beacon Light Rd.
Eagle, Idaho 83616
www.chatterboxinc.com

Printed in USA

ISBN 1-892326-15-9

TOPICS

Melody Ross

what TO write

Every family seems to have stories that are told generation after generation to define them, where they have come from, and where they are today. Sometimes the stories are comical, sometimes they are tragic. But the stories of everyday living and human struggle are what hold us all together decade after decade.

A few times a year, I find myself in my bedroom looking through the enormous, weatherworn antique trunk that is home to my old journals and memorabilia, my scrapbooks and the keepsakes of my grandparents. I pour through my handwritten thoughts noticing my ever-changing ink colors and handwriting ranging from hurried scribbles to clean, beautiful penmanship. I rediscover a confused young girl and a hopeful teenager. I shed a tear or two when I relive the fear and anxiety of new motherhood. I vow to try a little harder when I read about my great-grandparent's struggles while homesteading in America after a long, difficult trip from Germany. My heart warms when I read the words I wrote just after meeting my husband. Even then, it was "love at first sight".

I have been an avid journal, photo and memorabilia keeper since I was a pre-teen, and I am so thankful for the words that make sense of where and who I am now. Many of the words I have written over the past 20 years have been with the express purpose of documenting my true life. I want my children, grandchildren, and other people in my life to be able to understand and relate to it.

You may be the only person in your family or circle of friends who will take the time to write the important details and feelings of events and relationships. Whether you are writing about mistakes made, victories earned, or simply documenting your feelings about your loved ones, your words will be priceless to you and will help others piece together their own stories. Sometimes what you're writing may seem trivial at the time, but later on, you'll find that the little things are what tie us all together through the generations. Young children in your life may have little memory of their growing-up years without someone taking the time to archive the extraordinary, as well as typical moments, that characterize who they are.

My goal is that this book will inspire you to write things in your scrapbooks that you haven't thought of writing before, or to motivate you to write the things which you've always known that you need to write. Whether you are doing it for yourself, for your children or other family members, for friends, for the love of your life, or for future generations, documenting your part in the circle of humanity is one of the most important jobs that you will ever do.

Read through the creative journaling ideas ahead, and enjoy the examples from the exquisitely talented scrapbook designers. Put yourself into each of the stories and see how you might be able to write your own spectacular stories that will continue to be told long after you are gone.

As always, Make it Meaningful!

Melody Ross

Melody Ross

delegated JOURNALING

delegated JOURNALING

Sometimes you just get tired of doing it all yourself, right? A great solution to this dilemma is to delegate the journaling portion of your scrapbooking to others involved.

If you're doing a page about your vacation, invite your travel companion to write their favorite parts of the trip. If you're making an album about your son's graduation, ask his best friend write out memories from their senior year. If you are doing a project about your grandparents, have all of your siblings and cousins write what they remember about them. Convince your spouse to write down feelings about when your children were born. Request that your parents write down what they remember about you as a child if you are trying to do your personal history.

Think about the ways you can involve others in your scrapbooking projects. Look at the photos you are scrapbooking and see if there are people in those photos who can help you reminisce and capture those memories from a different angle.

Provide your delegates with the paper and pen that you want used if you are going to have them handwrite the journaling. If you plan to type it, have them email it to you so that you don't have to retype what they have already written.

The great part of delegating the journaling is that you often get more accurate information than if you would have done it yourself, and you definitely get a different point of view. It's also fun because it makes scrapbooking interactive, and everything is more fun when you can share it.

Sample Request:

I am creating a memory album about our trip to Hawaii. Would you take a few minutes and write about the following things?
-What was your favorite part of the trip?
-What was the most exciting thing we did?
-What would you definitely do again?
-What do you wish we would have taken photos of that we didn't?
Thanks for doing this for me. If you could just email me the answers, that would be great! I can't wait to share the finished scrapbook with you!

Most people will be happy to help you out, especially if you promise to show them your finished work, or maybe even make a copy for them. You might have to remind them or ask them to have it to you by a specific date.

This is a great way to add variety to your journaling, and to get a lot more done by 'sharing the load' of your scrapbooking. You'll wonder why you didn't try it before!

My Mother

by Jessi Stringham

1. **SUPPLIES:** Patterned Paper: Sitting Room: Small Sitting Plaid, Sitting Flowers, Light Sitting Stripe; Cardstock: Taupe (Bazzill); Love Tiles: My Mother; Rivets: Antique Bronze; Other: Ribbon: MayArts (polka dots), silk ribbon (source unknown); Making Memories date stamp; Canvas Paper (source unknown); Ink: Ranger Industries–Distress Ink

2. **TIP:** I created a tab for each section of journaling that my husband did about his mother. It is a fun and different way to do journaling, and it allows you to write more that way and include it all on the layout.

3. **MAKE IT MEANINGFUL:** For Mother's Day, I wanted my husband to document all of the different reasons that he loved and appreciated his mother. It was simple to get started because I had him use the topics on the Chatterbox Love as a starting point. It took him less than ten minutes to come up with his thoughts, and his mother enjoyed them forever!

Proud of her

by Jayla Campbell

1. **SUPPLIES:** Patterned Paper: Sitting Room: Small Sitting Plaid, Light Sitting Stripe; Love: My Mother, Tacks: Black Round; Other: Brown Cardstock, Ribbon

2. **TIP:** Use the Love Tiles to inspire yourself on what to interview someone else about.

3. **MAKE IT MEANINGFUL:** Cody has so much love and respect for his mother. This is something I saw in him before we were even married. He absolutely loved this picture taken candidly on our wedding day. I wanted to have him share why he is so proud of her.

The Dodge Truck

by Brooke Campbell

1. **SUPPLIES:** Patterned Paper: Den: Denim Stripes, Cardstock: Dark Denim Solid; Rivets: Silver; Other: clear vellum, wire, nails, black chalk, and Americana BT font

2. **TIP:** Use nails or other found objects on the page.

3. **MAKE IT MEANINGFUL:** When my husband left for the Army Reserves I wanted to surprise him with something when he got back. I asked him to write about what I did for him.

Mom

by Jlyne Hanback

1. **SUPPLIES:** Patterned Paper: Den: Den Blocks, Reading Room: Spruce Gerbers Vellum; Tacks: Denim Flower; Address Stickers: Spruce; Other: Staz-On ink in Olive Green by Tsukineko, twill tape: unknown

2. **TIP:** Use patterned vellum as an overlay on top of patterned paper for an interesting patterned effect.

3. **MAKE IT MEANINGFUL:** I asked my twelve year old son, Matthew, to look at the photographs of us and write down his feelings. I incorporated his actual hand written journaling into my layout. He chose to write about what I mean to him as a mom, and he included his favorite qualities about me in the journaling.

My Mother

by Jayla Campbell

1. **SUPPLIES:** Patterned Paper: Reading Room: Reading Flowers (front and back), Small Reading Stripe; Cardstock: Light Sand; Rivets: Antique Bronze; Tacks: Antique Bronze Round; Other: canvas, string pearls, button, Stamps-Hero Arts

2. **TIP:** Ask a parent to journal their childhood memories. Not only will it be fun for you, but also for generations to come, especially as times continue to change.

3. **MAKE IT MEANINGFUL:** When I was a little girl I would ask my mom and dad to tell me stories about their childhood. This would happen almost on a daily basis. I loved to hear the same stories over and over. These were my bedtime stories. With this page, I wanted to be sure to have my mom write her childhood memories, so I would never forget those stories I loved to hear so much.

Portrait of a Boy

by Robin Hohenstern

1. **SUPPLIES:** Patterned Paper: Den: Big Den Plaid (back), Den Weave, Big Den Stripes; Rec Room: Denim Stars (back); Rivets: Antique Bronze; Misc: Buttons; Script Stamp: Inkadoo; Black dye Ink: Memories; Rubber Stampede: Brown Pigment Ink; walnut ink; plain tag; mesh; rick-rack: Wrights; Dymo label; date stamp: Office Depot; compass; skeleton leaf

2. **TIP:** To place the rivets, I use a regular office punch. Then I take my Fiskars microtip scissors, and cut an "X" pattern over the punched area to make the paper "move over" for the rivet.

3. **MAKE IT MEANINGFUL:** My son had a project for school—to write about himself. He came home and did this on his computer in a cool cursive font and everything! The original printout is behind his picture.

Belly Laugh
by Heather Melzer

1. **SUPPLIES:** Patterned Paper: Cabin: Olive Daisy, Cabin Stripe; Cardstock: Dark Burgundy, Light Fawn; Frames: Cabin, Gallery Black; Tacks: Burgundy Round; Address Stickers: Black; Misc: black linen cardstock, ribbon by Offray, Zig Marker

2. **TIP:** Arrange three frames vertically on top of a strip of ribbon and tie a bow at the top to make them appear as if they are hanging on a wall.

3. **MAKE IT MEANINGFUL:** Have the subject of your photos journal about what they were thinking and feeling at the time the photos were taken. On this layout, I had my husband handwrite about spending quality time with our daughter while watching television, and about how he loves to make her laugh.

I Like Pumpkins Because...
by Tarri Botwinski

1. **SUPPLIES:** Patterned Paper: Sun Room: Sun Room Stripe; Cardstock: Dark Tangerine, Light Scarlet; Rivets: Antique Bronze; I.D. Tags: Scarlet; Tacks: Scarlet Round; Molding: Scarlet; Address Stickers: Black, Black Chippy; Misc: Fiber: Fibers By The Yard; Acrylic Paint: Delta Cinnamon; Dymo Label Maker

2. **TIP:** I dry brushed acrylic paint over Walls and Molding. On the tags, I folded them so the paint would stay in the creases for a different effect.

3. **MAKE IT MEANINGFUL:** I love to ask my children questions because their answers vary so much, depending on their age. I asked them why they liked pumpkins and incorporated their answers into a layout. I know they will look back on this and laugh as much as I do

United in Love

by Brooke Campbell

1. **SUPPLIES:** Patterned Paper: Cabin: Olive Daisy Vellum; Cardstock: Dark Olive; Rivets: Olive; Other: white thread, Hero Arts stamps, ColorBox black pigment brush pad, Doodle Basic font, and Times New Roman font

2. **TIP:** Scrapbook old pictures so you can remember your ancestors.

3. **MAKE IT MEANINGFUL:** My Grandparents recently had their 50th wedding anniversary. They each shared the story of how they met. I recorded it so that I can always remember their fun stories.

Madi K

By Melody Ross

1. **SUPPLIES:** Patterned Paper: Cottage: Rosey Bouquet; Cardstock: Chocolate (Bazzill); Rivets: Rosey; Font: Chatterbox- Heber; Others: ribbon, rick-rack white photo corners

2. **TIP:** Let your children answer your questions and type out the answers on their own.

3. **MAKE IT MEANINGFUL:** I let Madi type out the answers to this question and then let her cut it out on her own. My inspiration for doing this page came after finding her daydreaming at the breakfast table in her nightgown. I snapped a photo of her and knew that it was a perfect moment to get into her brain.

from 1978 to 2003 . . .

true love never grows old

Rick & Jill Steed were
married in the
Salt Lake temple
January 18, 1978.
They have had 5 children
& have started a
gr__ legacy together.

then & NOW

then & NOW

Close your eyes and think about yourself as a child. What did you think it would be like to be grown-up? Think back 5 years…what did you think you would be doing right now? Think about when you were single. What did you think marriage would be like? When you were younger, what did you think you would do for a living? Where did you think your life would take you? Are you the person you thought you would be?

Think about the way that you perceived things…education, rules, relationships…and compare them to what you know now.

It's always fun to see how far you have come in life, and it's a terrific way to report your progress in life, as well as your changing opinions, tastes and values. Here are some ideas to get you started.

Answer these questions and you'll get inspiration for meaningful and fun layouts!

1. My favorite weekend activity used to be _____. Now it's _____.

2. I was sure that someday I would _____, but now I'd never think of doing that.

3. I never thought I'd like to _____, but now it's one of my favorite things.

4. I could never understand people who would _____. Now I am one of them.

5. I thought I'd live in _____, but now I live in _____.

6. At one time, I felt very strongly about _____. My feelings have changed because _____.

7. Previously, what was most important to me was _____. Now what is most important to me is _____.

8. As a teenager, I lived to _____; these days, I live to _____.

9. The strongest word to describe me as a child was _____; the strongest word to describe me now is _____.

10. When I was younger, I thought my parents were _____; now I know my parents are _____.

11. I thought having _____ would bring _____ to my life; now I know it brings _____.

12. I was sure that married would be _____; I was surprised to learn it was _____.

13. When I started my career, I thought it would be _____; what it has turned out to be is actually _____.

14. I used to think success meant _____; now I know success really means _____.

15. At one time, I wanted to be known for _____; now I hope that people will recognize me for _____.

16. I thought having children would be _____; it has surprised me it is so _____.

17. I always thought happiness meant_____; now my happiness comes from_____.

18. ___years ago, my goals were_____; now my goals are_____.

Then & Now

by Robyn Werlich

1. **SUPPLIES:** Patterned Paper: Sitting Room: Sitting Flowers, Sitting Stripe, Small Sitting Stripe, Fawn Stripe; Cardstock: Dark Sand; I.D. Tags: Fawn; Tacks: Antique Gold Flower; Address Stickers: Spruce; Other: Marker from Stampin' Up!; Van Dyke Brown Ranger Ink, Jute, Safety Pin, Ribbon from Stampin' Up!; Burlap: Once Upon a Scribble

2. **TIP:** The Sitting Room collection was the perfect compliment for my thoughts on this page. It was soft and elegant and helped my mood carry on throughout the layout.

3. **MAKE IT MEANINGFUL:** Sometimes life doesn't turn out quite how you think it will. Life before a college degree was much different than life after. I wanted to document what I thought life would be like and how it turned out. Although it was much different than I expected, I believe it all happened for a reason.

Sebastian Then and Now

by Heather Melzer

1. **SUPPLIES:** Patterned Paper: Cottage Room: Butter Ticking, Butter Bouquet; Cardstock: Light Butter; Tacks: White Flower; Address Stickers: Tangerine; I.D. Tags: Taupe; Misc: white twill tape, white linen cardstock, pop dots, Dymo label gun; Font: Rickety, downloaded from www.twopeasinabucket.com

2. **TIP:** Thread twill tape through two I.D. Tags to form a border between two sheets of patterned paper.

3. **MAKE IT MEANINGFUL:** I included details about our Old English Sheepdog, Sebastian, at 8 weeks old and 2 years old. I included physical and personality traits from "then" and "now".

Then and Now

by Heather Preckel

1. **SUPPLIES:** Patterned Paper: Great Room: Chocolate Bloom, Scarlet Bloom, Great Plaid, Great Olive Stripe; Cardstock: Light Sand; Molding: Fawn; Nails: Olive; Other: Charms: JustJhone; Ribbon: Offray; Zig Writer: EK Success; Stencil: Decorcal, Inc; Van Dyke Brown Ink-Ranger; Transparency: 3M; Font: Attic downloaded from the Internet

2. **TIP:** Cut paper into different angles and place on background paper; put paper behind stencil so it peeks through; ink edges of paper for a little aged look.

3. **MAKE IT MEANINGFUL:** I am forever amazed at how fast my little girl has grown and this layout captures the heart of that for me. Motherhood has been a gift that has blessed my life beyond measure. Journaling: I am absolutely amazed at how fast time has flown since the day my husband and I first saw our new baby girl! How we had waited so long for her and it seemed that she came so quickly and our waiting was over…I love my sweet Kiersten, as much now as I did then!

True Love Never Grows Old

by Brooke Campbell

1. **SUPPLIES:** Patterned Paper: Great Room: Scarlet Bloom; Cardstock: Dark Olive, Black (Bazzill); Tacks: Olive Round; Other: white netting; white cardstock; Font: Formal Script; ColorBox Amber Clay fluid chalk inkpad

2. **TIP:** Use chalk around the edges so that the white paper doesn't stand out as much.

3. **MAKE IT MEANINGFUL:** My parents have been married for 25 years. They have been a great example to me because they have had such a great marriage. I did a simple timeline to show how they are still just as much in love today as they were before.

Me Then and Now

by Robin Hohenstern

1. **SUPPLIES:** Patterned Paper: Billiard Pinstripes; Cardstock: Dark Fawn; Love Tiles: Parlor; Nails: Fawn; Misc: Ribbon: vintage (brand unknown); Font: Decker (bold)

2. **TIP:** Use things from outside your "room" if the colors look good together (i.e. Love from Parlor used with Billiard).

   OR To adhere the vellum, use a glue stick under the pictures where it won't show. To adhere the black photo corners to the vellum, use a mini glue dot.

3. **MAKE IT MEANINGFUL:** With this topic, I wanted to choose photographs that represented completely different times in my life. In the first picture, I am with my best friend getting ready to go out to a Halloween party in college. In the second picture, I am with my husband and children. I love the contrast shown here, and of course, prefer "me now" to "me then".

- 1988 - 20 years old
- single party girl
- pharmacy student
- loved high heels and short skirts
- loved straight-legged jeans
- curly hair (naturally curly)
- more brunette than blonde
- drove a 1982 Buick Skylark
- lived in a dump with 3 friends in Moorhead, MN
- messy house-keeper
- never heard of scrapbooking
- cared more about my friends than family

- 2003 - 35 years old
- wife and mother
- pharmacist
- love clogs and long skirts
- love flare-legged jeans
- straightened hair (fighting nature)
- more blonde than brunette
- drive a 2001 Oldsmobile Silhouette
- live in a nice house with my 3 favorite people in Brooklyn Park, MN
- neat freak
- scrapbooking addict
- care more about my family than friends

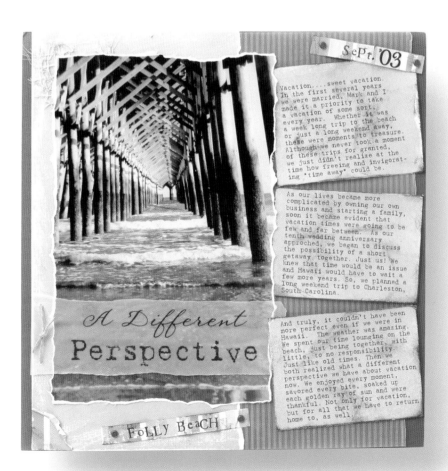

A Different Perspective

by Beth Hooper

1. **SUPPLIES:** Patterned Paper: Sitting Room: Sitting Room Stripe, Fawn Stripe Vellum; Cardstock: Light Denim, Light Sand; Tacks: Antique Gold; Address Stickers: Black; Other: Vellum: Bazzill; Cardstock: Bazzill (brown, textured); Hemp: manuf. Unknown; Stamping ink: Nick Bantock (Van Dyke Brown); Rubber stamps: PSX; Natural grass mesh: manuf. unknown; Fonts: Pegsanna, Harting (source unknown)

2. **TIP:** Age Chatterbox cardstock by sanding the edges to reveal the white core. Also, walnut ink may be spritzed on to age the cardstock as well.

3. **MAKE IT MEANINGFUL:** As I look back over the past ten years that Mark and I have been married, I realize there were things I took for granted. One of those being vacations. When we were able to take a much needed "mini vacation" this year, I had time to reflect upon how important those times were to me. I wanted to scrap book this occasion in terms of how things were then and how they are now. Although a lot of things have changed in our life, I wouldn't trade it now for a thousand vacations!

Then and Now
by Carolyn Peeler

1. **SUPPLIES:** Patterned Paper: Rec Room: Scarlet Posie, Cabin: Burgundy Daisy; Cardstock: Light Sand; I.D. Tags: Scarlet; Tacks: Scarlet Flower; Other: Photo Corners: Pioneer, Embroidery Floss: DMC; Acrylic Paint: Americana Sand and Delta Light Ivory; Alphabet Rubber Stamps: Hero Arts; Fonts: P22 Cezanne, CK Template, 2Peas Flea Market, 2Peas Katherine Ann; Ink: Stampin' Up!: Chocolate Chip, Creamy Caramel, Baroque Burgundy; Pen: Zig

2. **TIP:** I used acrylic paint to highlight the area I wanted to place the picture on the layout.

3. **MAKE IT MEANINGFUL:** I find it amazing when I look back to what I wanted to be when I was a small girl, that there are so many areas where I am doing what I dreamed. Although not all my dreams have been fulfilled exactly to the letter of what I envisioned, when it comes to the heart of it, I have accomplished a lot of what I thought I would. I am thankful for that.

Generaciones
by Kari Barrera

1. **SUPPLIES:** Patterned Paper: Cabin: Burgundy Daisy, Olive Daisy, Small Cabin Stripe, Gallery: Light Chocolate Open Dot; I.D. Tags: Burgundy; Nails: Black Round; Other: burlap, raffia

2. **TIP:** Adding elements such as raffia can really bring out the textural beauty in the paper design.

3. **MAKE IT MEANINGFUL:** I chose to do this layout in my broken Spanish. As my husband Greyson's family is Mexican, we want our children to celebrate this part of their heritage. This layout is about how when Greyson's Great Grandmother and he are together they represent both the past, and the future of the family.

Journaling Translation:
Generation to generation, Grandmother to Grandson. Together you are our family's past and future all in one moment. The then and now, the past and the future. Through Abuelita's eyes, we can see the past and all the history and strength that this family embodies, and through your eyes we can see the future and all it has to hold for both you and your children after you. Moments when they come together are a treasure to be embraced.

the DESIGNERS

Carrie Utley

My father passed away four years ago, and that event changed my whole outlook on life. I suddenly realized that things I had taken for granted, stories that I had become so used to hearing, would never be told again. All of his opinions, hopes, dreams, his entire HISTORY, are now at the mercy of failing memories and busy schedules. My father had a definite impact upon who I am and the choices that I've made. I scrapbook so I will never forget those everyday things...just our life as we see it and live it, uncensored and unembellished.

Leah Fung

I love scrapbooking! Scrapbooking combines all of my favorite things: photography, arts and crafts, journaling, and most important of all...my family. To me, scrapbooking is so much more than just capturing family events, like vacations and holidays. It's an opportunity for me to share my values, thoughts, and hopes with those I love. And through scrapbooking, I can capture all these things in a fun and creative way that makes it even more meaningful.

Annie Weis

I have become obsessed with paper, ribbon, stamps, inks, and any fun embellishment I can find. But my passion is not just about scrapbooking products; I love being able to call myself a creative person. Although I appreciate how much each page means to my family, what I really love is the creative process of making a page. Every time I feel inspired, learn a new technique, then create a layout I can share, I feel completely happy. Scrapbooking has enriched my life with creativity, friendship, and joy.

Christy Tomlinson

My mother has always encouraged me to write down in journals important events in my life, as well as everyday things I wanted to remember. Now that I am older and have children of my own, I realize how important those journals are to my children and me. Scrapbooking has become another way for me to document those important events in my life as well as my families. It allows me not only to write my feelings of these events, but also express through creativity the true meaning behind the pictures. Scrapbooking allows me to leave a legacy of the "real" me.

Beth Hooper

Photographs freeze moments in time. Moments that I want to savor, remember and cherish. Scrapbooking those moments is such a gratifying experience. I love scrapbooking because it is not only an excellent way to preserve cherished memories, but it is also a beautiful work of art. It makes me so happy to look at a completed layout and realize that generations from now, my family will be enjoying these pages also.

Dana Smith

Preserving the past is what it's all about. Not only with pictures, but more importantly, with words. Since I began my passion with scrapbooking, I have learned that a photo can tell a thousand words; but the journaling is priceless. Creating a page that not only has pictures but meaningful words is a gift that I give my children every time I finish a page. They may not appreciate it now, but I know that in the years to come, the memories of my past and that of my family will be preserved forever.

FAVORITES

Life is an opportunity, benefit from it.
Life is beauty, admire it.
Life is bliss, taste it.
Life is a dream, realize it.
Life is a challenge, meet it.
Life is a duty, complete it.
Life is a game, play it.
Life is a promise, fulfill it.
Life is sorrow, overcome it.
Life is a song, sing it.
Life is a struggle, accept it.
Life is a tragedy, confront it.
Life is an adventure, dare it.
Life is luck, make it.

Life is life, fight for it.

Life

When I found out that Hans had cancer, I decided to make a book for him, filled with words and images that would give him strength and hope. I used this quotation on the final page, because I thought it spoke so well to his good and bad fortune in life. Every time I read the quote, it filled me with resolution and energy, and I hoped these words would do the same for Hans. The quotation has been attributed to Mother Teresa, and even though I doubt that this is true, I liked the idea that I could include her in my father-in-law's book. There are few people who can match Mother Teresa's strength, devotion, generosity, and willpower, and I knew Hans would appreciate the wisdom of this devout woman. It has been said that Mother Teresa's whole existence was "a hymn to life," and this is exactly how I read these words. Maybe she didn't write them, but it doesn't matter to me or to Hans. These words are filled with life, and I know they gave him strength during a difficult time. Unlike my own father, Hans survived cancer, and he is still healthy today. Maybe it was the quick intervention and the expert treatment he received. Maybe he survived because of his faith and desire to live. I'd like to believe in the power of words, and I hope this poem played a small part in his recovery. I know these are words that will also help me through difficult times I may still face: "life is life, fight for it."

FAVORITES

You can tell a lot about someone by asking them what their favorites are. Favorites are fun to talk, think, and write about. What's not to love about favorite things?

Because this is such a commonly written-about subject, you will need to think outside the box if you want it to be extraordinary. Any favorites are great, but there are lots of exciting ways to write about them and to create a memory project around them.

You can take almost any of the other journaling subjects in this book and apply them to writing about favorites, but here are even more ideas…

•Take the packaging off of all of your favorite foods and use it as background paper or embellishments. Write everything you love about those foods…the way they smell, the way they melt in your mouth, the way the wrapper sounds when you're tearing it off.

•Take the tags or labels off of your favorite clothes and use them in your layouts. When a favorite clothing item is worn out, cut out a piece and include it in your scrapbook. Write about all the things you've done in the clothes you love, where you bought them and how much you paid for them (wouldn't it be fun to read about your grandmother's favorite clothes had she done this?)

•Include a CD of your favorite songs in an album. Write about what makes you listen to this particular music and what it is that you like most about it. Make color copies of CD covers and include those with the layouts you do. Write out especially compelling words or choruses of songs that mean something to you and explain why.

•Make an album of your favorite things to do when you are happy, when you are sad, when you are bored, when you are afraid, when you are alone, when you are with a lot of people, on holidays, on weekends, before you go to bed, when you wake-up, etc. Take pictures of yourself doing those things, if you can, and write what you love about each of them.

•When writing about your favorite color, look up color analysis on the internet and print out what the meaning of your favorite color is. See where you can find parallels in your personality, and write about why you love your favorite color.

Write about your favorites even if you think they are silly or won't matter to anyone else. Ask your family what their favorites are and make a page about it.

In 10 years, in 25 years, in 50 years and in 100 years, this information will likely be everyone's FAVORITE part of your scrapbook!

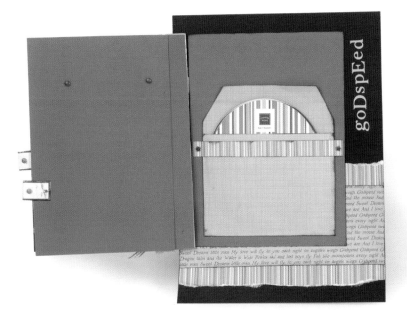

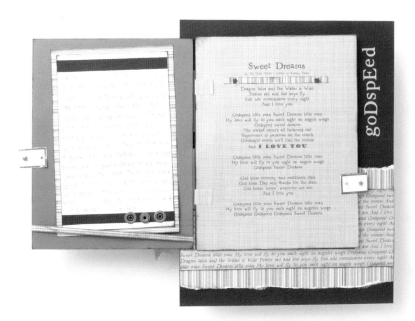

Sweet Dreams

by Jayla Campbell

1. **SUPPLIES:** Patterned Paper: Den: Light Den Stripe, Cabin: Olive Daisy; Cardstock: Denim (Bazzill), Brown (Bazzill), Tags: Denim; Tacks: Silver Star, Antique Bronze Star; Rivets: Olive; Address Stickers: Olive; Other: Ribbon, Silver Star (unknown)

2. **TIP:** Create more room to journal on a page by adding a small booklet.

3. **MAKE IT MEANINGFUL:** This song never meant quite so much to me until I had a little man of my own. This song is so soft and sweet and is played a lot at our house. It can bring tears to my eyes when I hear it because it reminds me of when my son Cole was little.

Remember...

by Brooke Campbell

1. **SUPPLIES:** Patterned Paper: Powder Room: Rosey Posie Vellum, Rosey Stripe Vellum; Cardstock: Light Rosey, Address Stickers: White; Nails: Clear Round; Other: DJ Basic font, and white ribbon

2. **TIP:** Layer many different sheets of paper.

3. **MAKE IT MEANINGFUL:** I found this little quote to remind me of some of the simple things on my wedding day.

Mornings With Joni

by Kari Barrera

1. **SUPPLIES:** Patterned Paper: Gallery: Small Black Gallery Dot, Dark Gallrey Blossoms, Black Gallery Blossoms, Gallery Skinny Stripe, Sitting room: Fawn Stripe; Cardstock: Fawn, Address Stickers: Chippy Circles Black, Butter, White; Other: butter fly (fake) buttons, Bazzill Brown Cardstock

2. **TIP:** Using black ink to trace over the letter stickers can help bring them out for titles.

3. **MAKE IT MEANINGFUL:** I wanted to record one of the simple pleasures I enjoy as a daily ritual: starting my days listening to Joni Mitchell, and enjoying our garden. It centers me and prepares me for my regular daily routine. I can imagine my kids hearing this album and thinking of me walking around in my robe and singing off-key.

LIFE

by Ann-Marie Weis

1. **SUPPLIES:** Patterned Paper: Billiard: Billard Pinstripes (back), Cabin: Olive Daisy (back), Gallery: Dark Chocolate Gallery Dot, Gallery Skinny Stripe; Cardstock: Dark burgundy; Foundations: Olive; Other: transparency film (for title) by Office Max; key and wire: source unknown; homemade wax seal; heart charm: source unknown, Silk ribbon source unknown; Fonts: Aramis, Lucida Sans Unicode, Lassigue D'Mato, downloaded from the Internet

2. **TIP:** I cut out a frame from the olive foundations and layered it with solid and patterned walls for a photo mat. To add more texture, I arranged ribbons underneath the photo mat in a design similar to the ribbon at the bottom right corner.

3. **MAKE IT MEANINGFUL:** I used this verse in a gift album for my father-in-law, and since I no longer have this album, I decided to make a page about it for myself. It reminds me of this powerful quotation and the impact it had on my father-in-law's life during a difficult time in both of our lives.

Amazing Grace

by Tarri Botwinski

1. **SUPPLIES:** Patterned Paper: Great Room: Great Room Floral, Great Little Stripes, Butter Bloom; Cardstock: Dark Olive, Dark Butter; I.D. Tags: Scarlet; Address Stickers: Olive; Molding: Scarlet; Tacks: Olive Round; Rivets: Scarlet; Other: Tulle; Floss: DMC; Fonts: Marydale and English from Internet

2. **TIP:** I used soft colored papers and lightly inked them to give the layout "babyish" feel. I mounted Address Stickers on squares to make them "pop".

3. **MAKE IT MEANINGFUL:** When my first born, Riley, was a baby, I sang *Amazing Grace* to him as a lullaby. When my other son and daughter arrived, I sang it to them too. Even now, when they need a little TLC, they ask me to sing *Amazing Grace*.

"You are My Sunshine"
by Beth Hooper

1. **SUPPLIES:** Patterned Paper: Gallery: Light Gallery Blossom, Cottage: Butter Ticking, Sitting Room: Fawn Stripe Vellum; Cardstock: Light Butter; Molding: Taupe; Frame: Gallery Black; Tacks: round black; Address Stickers: Black; Other: cardstock: Bazzill textured (brown); transparency: IBM; metal rimmed tag: Avery; brown and white gingham ribbon: Manuf. Unknown; stamping ink: Nick Bantock (Van Dyke Brown), Versa mark (clear); rubber stamp: PSX; fonts: Harting (source unknown), 2Peas Hot Chocolate, and 2Peas Blessing: www.twopeasinabucket.com

2. **TIP:** Solid Chatterbox cardstock has been stamped with a sunflower stamp using VersaMark ink.

3. **MAKE IT MEANINGFUL:** My mother used to sing *You are My Sunshine* to me when I was growing up. So, naturally, when I had Meredith, I began to sing this song to her. I would always sing this particular song to her while I rocked her to sleep. Now, whenever she needs a little extra TLC she will ask me to sing *You are My Sunshine*. I hope, when she becomes a mom, she will carry on the tradition of singing this song as well.

If You Could See What I See
by Heather Preckel

1. **SUPPLIES:** Patterned Paper: Cottage: Sky Cottage, Sky & Rosey Stripe, Great Room: Chocolate Bloom; Cardstock: Light Fawn Solid; Molding: Fawn; Nails: Fawn; I.D. Tags: Fawn; Other: household twine: unknown; ribbon: Offray; Zig Writer: EK Success; Fonts: Hanibal Lector and Attic downloaded from scrapvillage.com, P-22 Cezanne; Van Dyke Brown-Ranger

2. **TIP:** Cut paper in 6 inch squares and fan out behind picture and attach with Scrapbook Nails; cut different papers into 3 x 3 squares and place them in a row on the bottom of the cardstock; tie I.D. Tags around the journaling with household twine.

3. **MAKE IT MEANINGFUL:** My husband and I have been married for 10 years and sometimes it feels just like yesterday we said "I do." Steve loves to sing and he sings to me all the time.

Our Song

by Carolyn Peeler

1. **SUPPLIES:** Patterned Paper: Den: Light Den Stripe, Cabin: Burgundy Daisy, Cabin Stripe Vellum, Reading Room: Spruce Gerbers; Cardstock: Light Sand; Address Stickers: Taupe; Other: Vanilla Cardstock; Tag: Avery; Ink: Ancient Page Sandalwood and Stampin' Up! Chocolate Chip; Font: Times New Roman; Ribbon: Ofray, Button: Dollar Store; Letter Stamps: PSX

2. **TIP:** To mute the colors on the Cabin Stripe Vellum, I used the reverse side of it.

3. **MAKE IT MEANINGFUL:** When going through all the songs that have meant something to my husband and me, the song *The Other Side of Me* is always at the top of my list. I first heard this song when I was living in Holland and my husband was living in Canada. The words of this song are so powerful to me because they speak of how much a couple loves each other and how they don't want to be parted. To this day, I always get a melancholy feeling when I hear it.

Albert Einstein

by Leah Fung

1. **SUPPLIES:** Patterned Paper: Billiard Room: Billiard Room Plaid, Sitting Room: Fawn Stripe; Frames: Billiard Room; Address Stickers: Black; Tacks: Antique Silver; Nails: Black; Molding: Black; Other: Buttons, Fiber, Metal Plate, Thread, Chalk, Hero Arts Stamps, StazOn Ink; Font: Times New Roman

2. **TIP:** I mounted the frames on cardboard before adhering them to the layout to give them added dimension.

3. **MAKE IT MEANINGFUL:** I shared some of my favorite quotes with my kids and described what each of them mean to me and why I value them. The quotes also came from someone I admire, so I wanted to share these with them because doing so says a little about me too.

Favorite Quote

by Amy Yingling

1. **SUPPLIES:** Patterned Paper: Sitting Room: Sitting Flowers; Cardstock: Light Denim; ID Tags: Olive; Address Stickers: Black Chippy Circles; Rivets: Black, Antique Bronze

2. **TIP:** Use strips of paper to create pockets for texture and dimension. They are also a great place to hide pictures and journaling.

3. **MAKE IT MEANINGFUL:** Using a quote for your journaling is a great way to scrapbook your family values and the things you love.

Songs

by Mellette Berezoski

1. **SUPPLIES:** Patterned Paper: Sitting Room: Sitting Flowers and Fawn Stripe Vellum; Cardstock: Light Sand and Light Denim; Tacks: Round Antique Bronze; Molding: Denim; I.D. Tags: Fawn; Address Stickers: Sand and Denim; Other: photo corners by KOLO, ribbon by Offray, heart charms from old costume jewelry; Fonts: CAC Shishoni Brush, P-22 Cezanne, Broadcast, AvantGarde downloaded from the Internet

2. **TIP:** Cut and sew a page protector to the layout to create pocket windows for the journaling tags.

3. **MAKE IT MEANINGFUL:** I wanted to remember the songs that have always meant so much to my husband and me. I included the title of each song as well as the artist who performed it on the front of each tag. A short verse from each song is printed on the back of the tags. The tags fit into the clear pockets and can be removed and flipped over to the back.

the DESIGNERS

Brooke Campbell

Scrapbooking is one of my favorite hobbies, but there is so much more to it then just a fun pastime. It is a way to freeze all of my family's memories in time. I love to look back over the pages and remember all the wonderful things that have happened. A picture can sometimes say so much more then words. It is easier to use to tell a story then trying to write everything down.

Tari Botwinski

I have always kept scrapbooks and photo albums. After the birth of my son, Riley, I discovered the "new" style of scrapbooking and I was hooked! It is so important to me to record the little things in my family's life. We always remember the big things - first steps, birthdays, and holidays. But I love to record the small things: Quinn's love of worms, Jameson's collection of wood, or other things we might one day forget. I love doing crafts and working with my hands, and scrapbooking fills the need to create.

Candi Gershon

Scrapbooking is an important way for me to record my family's memories. I love photographs from when I was a child, but I have always wondered what the story was behind them. Through scrapbooking I can leave this information (not only the great photos documenting our lives, but the stories behind them) for my family. One day when my children have children of their own, they can share these memories and pass them down through generations - memories about their childhood, and who their parents were. I am leaving a legacy.

Jen Bourgeault

What started out as a way to simply preserve my photos has turned into so much more. Through my scrapbook pages, I am able to share my innermost thoughts and feelings with my children. I am able to capture how sweet and precious our family life is. And most importantly, I know that these moments can always be cherished with just a flip of a page.

Desiree McClellen

I love every aspect of scrapbooking: the thought process of layout ideas, picking out unique color combinations and of course, getting to play with the multitude of embellishments available. Scrapbooking is also important to me because I get to document my son's life and everything that is includes. I want him to be able to look back and see what his and our lives included. Lastly, scrapbooking is important to me because it has led to my deeper love of photography. It wasn't until I started scrapbooking that it became more of an "integral" part of my life.

Jessi Stringham

When I was ten years old, my father passed away unexpectedly. Although I was old enough to remember him, I don't know how he felt about me. I wish I had something tangible that would help me know of his love for me. Scrapbooking has given me the ability to express my feelings for my husband and son, capturing their everyday silliness, our trials and tribulations, and our triumphs. Simply put... Scrapbooking is my heart on paper.

WORDS

Collette is my niece and I adore everything about her. The first time I met her, she was only eight years old. She was a HEADSTRONG, yet KIND and LOVING little girl. Ten years later, she has also grown to be a BEAUTIFUL young women who is SMART and DOWN-TO-EARTH with a very GENUINE heart . She loves working with those who are in need and takes special care to make those around her feel loved. She is such a wonderful example for my daughter and for me as well.

genuine

smart

loving

beautiful

B

WORDS

You can't have journaling without words, can you? Putting the right words together can generate an enormous impact in your journaling. There are many creative ways to use words without making them form sentences, however.

This journaling technique consists of listing a few words or masses of words that embody what you are trying to communicate. You may use words that describe feelings, character traits, personality traits, favorite things, etc.

Journaling in this fashion leaves a lot to the imagination of the reader; they can form their own sentences in their minds using the words you provided. It's fun because you get to extract the 'meat' of the journaling, and leave the rest to be personally interpreted.

Here are some words to get you started…

Personality traits:
Kind, nice, caring, gentle, thoughtful, compassionate, considerate, helpful, loving, sensitive, affectionate, tender, warm, romantic, sentimental, kind-hearted, smart, clever, intelligent, bright, brainy, sharp, gifted, outgoing, sociable, friendly, gregarious, extroverted, welcoming, gracious, pleasant, enjoyable, shy, reserved, timid, bashful, inhibited, quiet, humble, modest, unassuming, meek, unpretentious, funny, amusing, comical, witty, hilarious, neat, orderly, organized, methodical, systematic, logical, creative, innovative, visionary, dreamer, imaginative, resourceful, artistic

Character attributes:
Honest, truthful, sincere, trustworthy, candid, straightforward, upright, good, decent, reliable, scrupulous, honorable, admirable, worthy, praise-worthy, moral, principled, respectable, proper, steadfast, highly-regarded, unfailing, ethical, just, polite, courteous, loyal, faithful, responsible, dedicated, devoted, committed, conscientious, thorough, attentive, industrious, busy, productive, hardworking, diligent, resolute, sacrificing, persevering, encouraging, enduring, serene, tranquil, peaceful, quiet, still, passionate, wholehearted, eager, animated, energizing, ready, willing, raring-to-go, enthusiastic, broadminded, open-minded, patient, tolerant, balanced, understanding, charitable, accepting, perceptive, appreciative, supportive, grateful, thankful, generous, giving, altruistic, helpful, unselfish, humane, selfless, philanthropic, objective, fair, unbiased

Physical descriptions:
Beautiful, stunning, gorgeous, adorable, cute, eye-catching, colorful, rich, vivid, vibrant, lively, artistic, handsome, good-looking, attractive, tall, soaring, large, giant, small, tiny, petite, miniature, miniscule, alive, thriving, flourishing, blooming, round, spherical, curved, globular, square, angular, unique, distinctive, rare, unusual, bright, dazzling, brilliant, dark, dim, shady, shadowy, gloomy, sunny, cloudy, clear, picturesque, scenic, pleasing

Treasure this Day

by Ruth De Fauw

1. **SUPPLIES:** Patterned Paper: Den: Light Den Stripe, Den Blocks; Cardstock: Light Violet; Address Stickers: Denim, Fawn, Black Chippy Circles; Rub-ons; Other: Date Stamp; In: Versacolor; Embroidered Flowers; Diamond Glaze; Black and Sky Tags: Tags 2 Dye4- www.canscrapink.com; Ribbon: C.M. Offray & Sons Ltd.

2. **TIP:** Cut out the blocks on the patterned paper to create colorful journaling blocks and a modern design.

3. **MAKE IT MEANINGFUL:** Sometimes a photo can speak more for you than a five page essay. For this layout, I knew that only key words were necessary to describe the wonderful day we spent at the beach on Grandma De Fauw's Birthday.

Friends

by Jayla Campbell

1. **SUPPLIES:** Patterned Paper: Great Room: Butter Bloom, Butter & Olive Stripe; Cardstock: Light Butter; I.D. Tags: Spruce; Frames: Cabin; Tacks: Antique Bronze Round; Other: Ribbon: Stamps-Hero Arts

2. **TIP:** Use the I.D. Tags to make your words stand out on the page.

3. **MAKE IT MEANINGFUL:** I have been blessed with good friends who have supported me through everything. I love these girls!

Fresh

by Kari Barrera

1. **SUPPLIES:** Patterned Paper: Reading Room: Reading Diamond (Limited Edition), Spruce Gerber, Powder Room: Rosey Stripe (back), Rosey Posie Vellum, Tacks: White Flower, Pink Flower; Address Stickers: Black; Other: shipping tags: unknown. antique lace: local antique store; letter stencils: Chartpack; acrylic paint: Plaid (white) Gingham; ribbon: unknown; stamping ink: Memories (pink); metal photo corners: DiBona Designs; Dymo label maker; photo matte board: unknown; font: TwoPeas Falling Leaves-www.twopeasinabucket.com; quote: www.twopeasinabucket.com (author unknown)

2. **TIP:** Use Chatterbox tacks to anchor the stencils to the page. Change the color of the stencils easily by painting them with acrylic paint and then inking them with your choice of stamping ink (in this case, pink).

3. **MAKE IT MEANINGFUL:** I took this photo of Meredith a few days after celebrating my first Mother's Day. In fact, the flowers I made the halo out of were part of my Mother's Day bouquet. When I look at Meredith, I realize what a blessing it is to be her mother. I am so thankful that God saw fit to place her, a sweet new blossom of humanity, into my hands for safekeeping.

Our Little Boy

by Mellette Berezoski

1. **SUPPLIES:** Patterned Paper: Cabin: Olive Stripes and Olive Plaid; Cardstock: Dark Butter; Love Tiles: Den; Frames: Den and Rec Room; Molding: Olive; Nails: Butter; Address Stickers: Black; Other: leather lacing by Prym-Dritz, stamping ink by Clearsnap

2. **TIP:** Crumple and lightly sand patterned paper to create a more rustic, aged look.

3. **MAKE IT MEANINGFUL:** I took these photos of my son at my daughter's soccer game. He was so happy cheering for his sister that I wanted to journal the words and phrases I remember thinking to myself as I watched him that day.

A Childs Promise

by Vanessa Reyes

1. **SUPPLIES:** Patterned Paper: Rosey Bouquet, Light Powder Stripes, Black Gallery Swirl, Black Gallery Squares; Rivets: Cream; Nails: Rosey Round; Address Stickers: Rosey; Frames: Powder Room and Gallery Black; Other: metal rim tags; safety pins; photo flips: Making Memories; letter stamps: Ma Vinci; metal clips: limited editions; ribbons: Offray

2. **TIP:** Using fabric can be a fun way to add a little texture or pattern. Try using fabric swatches or fabric scraps to start out with.

3. **MAKE IT MEANINGFUL:** Hidden journaling has become one of my favorite ways to journal on a layout. It gives me so much freedom to express my most private feelings. I also like to use everyday pictures to go along with a personal letter or messages to be seen later by a loved one.

Dream

by Heather Preckel

1. **SUPPLIES:** Patterned Paper: Reading Room: Spruce Gerber, Holiday Plaid; Cardstock: Dark Olive; Nails: Clear Square. Rivets: Antique Bronze; Frames: Cabin; Chatterbox Paint Chip; Other: transparency: 3M; stamp: Journal Slab/Postmodern Design, Dream Stamp: Stampers Anonymous; Van Dyke Brown-Ranger; buttons: Goodwill, burlap: Foam and Fabric, ribbon: Ofray, tag: avery; household twine: Lowes

2. **TIP:** Ink the tag with brown ink for an aged look. Sand the edge of plaid paper. Journal on a transparency (cut just the tip of it and then tear it). Run strips of paper through Dymo label maker for your own embossed paper.

3. **MAKE IT MEANINGFUL:** Dream, Discover, and Destiny...all things I want my daughter to always have and do. I wanted this layout to speak my heart to her and hopes I have for her future. Journaling reads: I love to watch you DISCOVER this world around you....I pray you follow your DREAMS with all your heart...and fulfill the DESTINY you were put on this earth for!

Best Friends

by Kristi Baumgarten

1. **SUPPLIES:** Patterned Paper: Cabin: Olive Stripe; Cardstock: Dark Olive, Dark Scarlet; Address Stickers: (brother/sister); Other: mesh, ribbon, tag, safety pin, Dymo label maker; PSX stamps

2. **TIP:** Use words to describe your picture. I used stamps to say the words that describe Kyle and Chloe clowning around for the camera.

3. **MAKE IT MEANINGFUL:** Don't forget to record the silly, every day moments in your scrapbooks.

Mind Power

by Candi Gershon

1. **SUPPLIES:** Patterned Paper: Sun Room: Sunny Plaid, Pool Tiles, Den: Den Weave; Cardstock: Dark Scarlet; Tacks: Antique Bronze Round, I.D. Tags: Olive; Frames: Den; Address Stickers: Burgundy Chippy, Black; Other: Ink by Ranger, Colorbox; Fonts: LD Remington Portable, 2Peas Typo, LD Underwood 5, CK Chemistry, 2Peas Jack Frost, CK Daydream, Damned Architect, 2Peas High Tide, Impact, 39 Smooth, College Condensed, Stencil, X-Files

2. **TIP:** Enhance the Chatterbox Frames by adding a piece of patterned paper on the back (for a splash of color), and adhering with a 3-D Adhesive for added dimension.

3. **MAKE IT MEANINGFUL:** This picture of my son really captures what an intense thinker he can be. I simply wrote down the words that the picture brought to my mind and looked through a thesaurus to find similar words to convey the message. For fun, I included a small tag on the bottom with the date the photo was taken and a caption that reads "future genius".

Beautiful

by Christy Tomlinson

1. **SUPPLIES:** Patterned Paper: Reading Room: Soft Olive Stems, Soft Reading Stripe, Reading Poppies; Cardstock: Light Spruce (Bazzill); I.D. Tags: Spruce, Scarlet, and Taupe; Letter Stencil: Black; Rub-ons: Black Chippy; Other: Ink: Tim Holtz Distressed Ink by Ranger- Vintage photo and Antique Linen; Flower: Prima; Ribbon: Offray and Making Memories; Staples, and White Mesh; Fonts: Twopeas Tasklist (downloaded from the Internet) and Emmascript

2. **TIP:** Use Chatterbox I.D. Tags to create a title down the side of your page. Adding mesh to your page creates a look of dimension without the bulk. Ribbons create a feminine touch to any layout.

3. **MAKE IT MEANINGFUL:** Collette is my niece and I truly adore her. The first time I met her she was very young and feisty, but she was also so sweet and kind. Her father had just passed away, and although she was extremely sad, she had this sparkle in her eye. Years later she is still that same headstrong, sweet, kind, and loving girl. She is very smart, down-to-earth, and genuine. She loves working with people who suffer from mental and physical disabilities. She has so much patience for others and is always willing to help. She is not only beautiful on the outside, but on the inside as well.

Things I want to do in my lifetime (not in any particular order):

* are the things I have already accomplished

1. Travel the globe
2. Go to a prestigious university
3. Live life to the fullest*
   (I try really hard to do this every day)
4. Get straight A's even through college
5. Smile often*
   (I can't help it, I like to smile)
6. Laugh so hard I cry*
   (I can't help this either)
7. Write an award winning novel
8. Own a donor card
9. Play the oboe in a professional orchestra
10. Comfort someone*
    (my baby brother, my friends)
11. Buy a puppy
12. Make friends all around the world*
    (I have pen pals in Australia & Canada)
13. Stop racism wherever and whenever I can
14. Never break the law
15. Ride the tallest roller coaster in the world
16. Change someone's life forever*
    (my mom says I have already done this
    many times)

Written by Maysie, age 12 1/2   December 2003

iN My LiFetiMe

LISTS

LISTS

Are you a list person? List making is not only fun and easy to do, it also makes following and clearly understanding the information behind the writing much easier for the reader. Lists require very little sentence structure, very few words, and can be finished much more quickly than conventional or creative writing techniques.

Here's a LIST of list ideas!

-favorite songs
-things to do in your town
-reasons you love your family
-things that make you (or someone you adore) unique
-things you want to do in your lifetime
-things you have already done in your lifetime
-items found in your purse or car or desk
-things you purchase regularly
-things others may not know about you
-friends in your life
-favorite movies, or movies you have seen
-books you have read
-things you do in an average day
-places you have been

-people you admire
-names you are considering for your future children
-what you daydream about
-jobs or positions you have held
-your favorite foods
-your favorite restaurants
-people you have dated
-things you did for fun as a child
-funny 'first words' of your children (or children in your life)
-the most important days of your life
-websites you like to visit
-what you have done on your birthday since you were born
-what is hanging in your closet
-the places you have lived
-schools you have attended
-teachers you remember
-cars you have owned
-places you would love to visit
-words of advice for your children (or other loved ones in your life)
-your typical grocery shopping list
-goals you have for your children (or others in your life)
-your favorite scrapbooking (or any other hobby) supplies

In My Lifetime

by Mellette Berezoski

1. **SUPPLIES:** Walls Patterned: Great Room: Great Little Stripes and Scarlet Bloom; Cardstock: Light Butter; Molding: Olive; Nails: Round Butter; Rivets: Antique Gold; Other: floss, buttons, paper clips, and staples

2. **TIP:** Copy the flower on the pattern paper and hand stitch it for a fun accent. Finish off with a round nail in the center.

3. **MAKE IT MEANINGFUL:** I asked my daughter to write down a list of things she would like to do in her lifetime. I was surprised to get a list back that had so many noble and caring things written on it. I truly cherish this page because it so wonderfully displays not only her innocence, but her kind and giving heart as well.

...In Our Lifetime

by Heather Melzer

1. **SUPPLIES:** Patterned Paper: Sitting Room: Sitting Flowers, Fawn Stripe; Cardstock: Light Sand; I.D. Tags: Taupe; Other: Ribbon by Offray, Fonts: Pegsanna and Day Roman

2. **TIP:** Cut your patterned paper down to 8.5x11 size and print your title directly onto it. Then use a coordinating patterned paper as accents on the sides with ribbon to hide the seams.

3. **MAKE IT MEANINGFUL:** Ask your significant other to make a list of things he would like to do in his lifetime and make a list of your own as well. Include them on a layout with a photo of the two of you, or separate photos, for a keepsake you can look back on in years to come. It is also a great way to make sure you do all the things you hope to do.

So Many blessings in one little boy!

Forever Blessed

by Kari Barrera

1. **SUPPLIES:** Patterned Paper: Sitting Room: Sitting Stripe and Sitting Circles (Limited Edition), Den: Den Weave; I.D. Tags: Taupe; Address Stickers: Black, Denim Other: black ribbon by Offray

2. **TIP:** Reverse print on a transparency to get the title to go over several papers at once.

3. **MAKE IT MEANINGFUL:** Gavin is such a blessing to us. After a very difficult pregnancy, we are sure to take the time to be thankful for every little blessing that makes him who he is.

What I love about you

by Carolyn Peeler

1. **SUPPLIES:** Patterned Paper: Gallery: Big Gallery Stripe, Chocolate Gallery Swirl; Cardstock: Light Sand; Other: vellum: unknown; ribbon: Offray; fabric; waverly

2. **TIP:** I used some decorator fabric that matched the paper to add a different texture to the layout.

3. **MAKE IT MEANINGFUL:** I made a list consisting of the many things I love about my nephew Daniel.

This is me...then

by Carolyn Peeler

1. **SUPPLIES:** Patterned Paper: Powder Room: Rosey Posie, Rosey Stripe;Cardstock: Light Rosie; Other: Ribbon: Offray; Buckle: Dollar Store; Flower: Nature's Reflection; Pen: Zig; Number Stamps: Hero Arts; Brad: Dollar Store; Fonts: 2 Peas Flea Market, 4990810; Ink: Stampin' Up! Chocolate Chip and Basic Black; Acrylic Paint: Antique White

2. **TIP:** I took a fake flower off its stem and used glue dots to adhere it to the page in order to continue the feminine feeling of this layout.

3. **MAKE IT MEANINGFUL:** At this point in my life, with no children and an extremely flexible work schedule, I've realized that I will probably never have as much freedom to plan my days as I have right now. I decided to make a list of some of my favorite ways to spend my time, from shopping, to watching TV, to scrapbooking.

I have been blessed

by Amy Yingling

1. **SUPPLIES:** Patterned Paper: Cabin: Cabin Plaid, Small Cabin Stripe; Cardstock: Dark Olive, Dark Sand; Address Stickers: Scarlet; Tacks: Scarlet Flower; Rivets: Antique Bronze; Frames: Cabin; I.D. Tags: Burgundy; Other: Van Dyke brown stamp pad, antique alphabet stamp by PSX, Making Memories date stamp, ribbon, and twine

2. **TIP:** Use strips of paper to create your lists.

3. **MAKE IT MEANINGFUL:** I find myself feeling overwhelmed with gratitude at times, and I find that making a page is a great way to express how I feel that day. Make a list of your blessings, either about life in general, or specific to that day.

To Do

by Melanie Bauer

1. **SUPPLIES:** Patterned Paper: Den: Den Blocks; Cardstock: Dark Spruce, Dark Taupe; Nails: Spruce; I.D. Tags: Taupe; Address Stickers: Spruce and White; Other: Pen by Zig Millennium; Ribbon by Offray; Stamps by PSX and Hero Arts; Ink by Nick Bantock; Embroidery Floss by DMC; Metal Tags by Avery; Button by unknown

2. **TIP:** Use metal rimmed tags from an office supply store to spell out your title. To hyphenate a word, use a button.

3. **MAKE IT MEANINGFUL:** Thomas is a constant source of amusement and his lack of schedule makes my husband and me quite envious! Journaling all of the important things on his "to-do" list is a unique way to document his daily routine.

Counting my Blessings

by Robyn Werlich

1. **SUPPLIES:** Patterned Paper: Rec Room: Scarlet Butter Stripe; Cardstock: Butter, Scarlet, Spruce; I.D. Tags: Butter; Rivets: Antique Gold; Scrapbook Molding: Scarlet; Frames: Reading Room; Other: Marker from Stampin' Up!; Van Dyke Brown Ranger Ink; Hemp Rope; Alphabet stamps from Stamper's Anonymous; Walnut Ink

2. **TIP:** Intertwine the rope in between the holes of the molding as a fun accent to your layout. Spraying walnut ink on the papers can add a wonderful aged feel to your layout.

3. **MAKE IT MEANINGFUL:** I have been so blessed in my life. I wanted to capture my thoughts and what I considered to be blessings on a layout for my children. I wrote all my blessings, large and small, around the border of the page. It was a fun way to document my personal feelings and thoughts about the blessings in my life.

A Day in the Life of Me

by Desiree McClellan

1. **SUPPLIES:** Patterned Paper: Sitting Room: Light Sitting Stripe; I.D. Tags: Fawn; Nails: Taupe Square; Font: 2Peas Rickety (www.twopeasinabucket.com)

2. **TIP:** I printed directly on the ID Tags by running them through my printer.

3. **MAKE IT MEANINGFUL:** I wanted to document a typical day for my son in 2003. I thought it would be interesting for him to look back on this layout and see what life was like way back when.

One Day

by Ann-Marie Weis

1. **SUPPLIES:** Walls Patterned: Rec Room: Rec Blocks; Cardstock: Dark scarlet, Light Denim, Dark olive, Light fawn; Frames: Rec room; Other: Black Cardstock: source unknown; Fonts: Stamp Act and 2Peas Chestnut (downloaded from the Internet)

2. **TIP:** I cut wide strips of Chatterbox Cardstock and used a narrow strip of patterned paper (Rec Blocks) for a graphic, masculine look. The Rec Room circle frame is used to emphasize the keyword of the layout.

3. **MAKE IT MEANINGFUL:** I wanted to make a layout about some of my husband's dreams and hopes. Sometimes work and everyday life get him off track, and I wanted to give him something to help him focus. The layout is a way to show my support for his goals, even the ones that cannot be realized today or anytime soon.

memory JOGGING

first date

menu

Guru's
enlightened eating

Enlightened Salads
$3.99

Asian
Arranged enlightened lettuces topped with
orange segments, sprouts, shredded carrots,

GIVE & TAKE

Guru's

JaN

01

memory JOGGING

Memory Jogging is simply interviewing yourself to remember details you may not have otherwise remembered, or unearthing forgotten pieces of your past. There are many things you may take for granted now, but will be of tremendous sentimental value to you later.

The easiest way to utilize this technique is to study your photographs and memorabilia. I think of a photo of my parents in their third year of marriage in 1969. In this photo, my oldest brother at age two is sitting with them on a bench in front of their little home, and my mother has curlers in her hair, covered with a sheer scarf. My father has his arm around my mother, with his typical attire of a plaid button-up shirt and slacks with Juicy Fruit gum and a Bic pen in his shirt pocket. It is a picture of perfect happiness, with such utter contentment on their faces you can almost smell the clean air they must have been breathing. This photo has always been very compelling to me, as it tells the story of 'starting out' in life and in marriage. While looking at it a few years ago, I noticed something very subtle I hadn't noticed before.

In the photo, my parents and brother are sitting in front of the large living room window. In the reflection of the window, you can see a car that is parked in front of the house. I asked my father about this car, and as it turns out, it was their first car, a model-T Ford. My father was so thrilled he could look at that photo and see his old car, which he has no other photo of. I'm sure when this photo was taken, the reflection was not even noticed, but now it is "buried treasure" unearthed.

Look through your own photos and see what kind of treasures you can find! In photos that you have not seen in a long time, you are likely to see people and details in the background that will make you remember things you may have misplaced in your mind.

Search for things written in the background, for clocks telling what time it was, for old technology lurking beside the people in the photos. Study clothing, food, and books that may be in the photos. Look at reflections, things sitting on tables, roadsigns and place-of-business signs. These things all tell a story of their own and at the least, spark your memory for a wonderful piece of journaling.

On the flip-side, try to take more photos with things like this in the background, so you can write about it in the future, too!

1ˢᵗ Apartment

by Jayla Campbell

1. **SUPPLIES:** Patterned Paper: Great Room: Great Little Stripe, Great Room Floral; Cardstock: Light Taupe; Frames: Sitting Room; Rivets: Antique Bronze; Address Stickers: Scarlet; Other: hemp cord

2. **TIP:** Be sure to add addresses to pages that have a specific location that you are journaling about.

3. **MAKE IT MEANINGFUL:** This is the apartment where we lived when we were first married. It will be fun to look back on this page later and remember where we started.

My Handwriting

by Robin Hohenstern

1. **SUPPLIES:** Patterned Paper: Parlor: Parlor Blossoms, Parlor Stripe; Cardstock: Violet; Address Stickers: Violet; Love Tiles: Parlor; Other: Ribbon: May Arts; photo holders from surplus store (Ax Man); machine sewing; date stamp: Office Depot; Pen: Zig writer

2. **TIP:** Use ribbon to hold the scrapbook love sayings.

   Or - if you'd like to move the stickers after they're down, take a push-pin and carefully (without tearing the paper) put it under the sticker until it comes off the page. Then reposition and smooth with the back (not sharp side) of the push pin. I use a fat rounded one and it works great!

3. **MAKE IT MEANINGFUL:** Right away, when I thought of "memory jogging exercises", I thought of my habit of writing on my hand. I do it all the time and I thought it would be fun to document it in a layout.

What I'll Miss... When You Grow Up!

by Amy Yingling

1. **SUPPLIES:** Patterned Paper: Sitting Room: Sitting Flowers and Small Sitting Plaid; Cardstock: Light Fawn and Dark Taupe; Frames: Den; Address: Fawn; Other: natural twine

2. **TIP:** Don't be afraid to stitch directly onto your photo to hold in place.

3. **MAKE IT MEANINGFUL:** Jog your memory by creating a list. I did *What I'll Miss When You Grow Up* and answered it in a list form.

Our Tree

by Dana Smith

1. **SUPPLIES:** Patterned Paper: Reading Room: Holiday Plaid; Love Tiles: Reading Room, Rivets: White; Molding: Olive; Tacks: White; Address Stickers: Black Chippy Circles; Other: Ribbon: Offray; Stencil: Office Depot; Ink: Memories

2. **TIP:** I placed pop dots under the moldings and then placed them over the photo of the tree. I completely covered the card board stencil with ink. I also attached rivets to the Love Tile, ran some ribbon through it, then attached it to layout.

3. **MAKE IT MEANINGFUL:** Ever since my husband and I have been married we have decorated our tree a day or two after Thanksgiving. I love traditions and this is one I treasure. The tree isn't what it used to be now that we have had children, but I still look forward to it just as much.

America Home That We Love

by Vanessa Reyes

1. **SUPPLIES:** Patterned Papers: Den: Den Blocks and Den Circles Vellum; Cardstock: Scarlet and Spruce; Love Tiles: Rec Room; Tacks: Denim Stars; Rivets: Scarlet; Molding: Fawn; Address Stickers: Black; Other: metal rim tag: Making Memories; compass: United Additions; stamps: Ma Vinci and Rubber Stampede; Paint: Delta

2. **TIP:** If you just can't find that perfect shade of cardstock, or the perfect patterned paper, try using paint as your medium. Paint can easily double as a texture or as a cardstock color.

3. **MAKE IT MEANINGFUL:** Fourth of July has always been one of my family's favorite holidays! Celebrating the land we love always gives me lots of inspiration, and a proud feeling in my heart. Even though most often those dark night-time pictures don't always turn out the best, simply using a flag, or any other piece of memorabilia, can be just as meaningful.

First Date

by Jayla Campbell

1. **SUPPLIES:** Patterned Paper: Sitting Room: Small Sitting Plaid, Gallery: Small Black Gallery Dot, Cabin: Small Olive Daisy Vellum; Cardstock: Light Spruce; Nails: Black Round; Rivets: Brushed Silver; Address Stickers: Black; Other: ribbon, charm, address plate, small clothespin, key tags, paper clip

2. **TIP:** Journal on a tag and stick it in an envelope on your page

3. **MAKE IT MEANINGFUL:** Cody and I bonded instantly on our first date. We talked all night long and seemed to have so much in common. I love to look back and remember how much fun it was getting to know him.

Unforgettable

by Kari Barrera

1. **SUPPLIES:** Patterned Paper: Sitting Room: Sitting Room Flowers; Cardstock: Dark Taupe; Address Stickers: Black; Frame: Olive; Other: gingham ribbon, organza ribbon, silk flowers, silver cross

2. **TIP:** Use the frames to showcase a special memento.

3. **MAKE IT MEANINGFUL:** My husband and I sat down over coffee and brainstormed all the little elements of our wedding day that we really enjoyed, the less than obvious wedding day memories. I then wrote our list onto the background paper. This page is now a treasure that documents the little details that we will never forget about our special day.

Love

by Rachel Ludwig

1. **SUPPLIES:** Patterned Paper: Cottage: Butter Ticking, Sky & Rosey Stripe; Cardstock: Light Denim, Dark Butter, Light Butter; I.D. Tags: Denim; Tacks: Butter Flower, Butter Round; Other: Magic Scraps Transparency; Dark blue textured paper (from a local stamp store that sells extra large sheets of paper); PSX Antique Lowercase stamps; Ribbon: unknown; Flowers from Walmart; Marvy 1122 LePlume II pen; Font: California FB

2. **TIP:** I folded the patterned paper along the bottom in different ways (vertically, horizontally and diagonally) to create creases. Then I sanded the creases to bring out the pattern I created. Each of these different pieces of paper is sewn onto the background cardstock. I Used Marvy 1122 LePlume II pen instead of ink for the stamps.

3. **MAKE IT MEANINGFUL:** When I was growing up, my grandparents lived next door to us. I have so many special memories of them. I hope that my son will also be able to experience a similar relationship with his grandparents, and grow up with many happy recollections of time spent with them.

My Yellow Dress

by Tarri Botwinski

1. **SUPPLIES:** Patterned Paper: Sitting Room: Small Sitting Plaid, Sitting Flowers, Den: Den Weave; Cardstock: Light Denim, Dark Denim, Dark Butter; Molding: Denim, Butter; Rivets: Butter; Address Stickers: Butter, Denim Chippy; Tacks: Butter Round, Denim Round, Denim Flower; Other: Fibers: Fibers By The Yard; Ink: Colorbox

2. **TIP:** I altered the photo so the focus would be on the dress. I tore, rolled, and inked the paper.

3. **MAKE IT MEANINGFUL:** The dress my daughter, Quinn, is wearing was my dress when I was little- My FAVORITE dress. My mother saved it and recently gave it to me. When my daughter saw it, she had to try it on. The photo is from that event.

Our Place

by Jessi Stringham

1. **SUPPLIES:** Patterned Paper: Great Room: Chocolate Bloom, Small Great Plaid, Great Little Stripe (reverse side), Dark Chocolate Stripe (reverse side), Great Plaid; Cardstock: Dark Olive, Light Olive; Address Stickers: Olive; Tacks: Olive; Other: ribbon (source unknown), charm (source unknown), push pin (source unknown), thin cork board, Making Memories rectangle tag; Fonts: Century Gothic; Ink: Ranger Industries– Distress Ink

2. **TIP:** For my journaling, I decided to make my own customized cork board using Chatterbox paper to have it stand out and be the focus on the layout. I had a picture of my husband and me that fit perfectly into the tag. I topped it off with a charm and some ribbon.

3. **MAKE IT MEANINGFUL:** Until I completed this layout, it was hard to imagine that my husband and I have known each other for twelve years. It was fun to look back in retrospect and recall our days of courtship. I was actually shocked this memory happened over ten years ago. But at the same time, it seemed just like yesterday. It was important to me to write my feelings of the time we shared back then. I'm not sure I would have articulated my feelings in the same way had I written about them ten years earlier. This shows how I've matured over the years, both emotionally and in the manner I capture my personal feelings.

five SENSES

YUMMY! YUMMY! [MM]MY! YUMMY! YUMMY! YUMM

Dayton

You don't even know how to read yet, but you start dancing in your carseat as soon as you SEE a sign that says "McDonald's", "Sonic", or "Dominos Pizza".

You can SMELL dinner cooking in the oven even when you are happily playing in the backyard.

You jump up and run to the kitchen every time you HEAR one of us opening the refrigerator door.

You try to TOUCH every single dish in the buffet line. we are thankful that Daddy is still much stronger than you.

You savor each bite as if you could TASTE heaven.

age 2 · June 2003

the Joy of eating

five SENSES

The first thing you'll learn in any creative writing class is to explore all of your senses and descriptively write about them.

It's easy! Just think what you're scrapbooking about, then think about what comes to mind in terms of what you see, touch, taste, hear, and smell. Include those things in your journaling, and you'll have some first class literature on your hands, as well as meaningful memories that won't be forgotten.

Here are some descriptive words for the five senses. Try them out and make a habit of including information about as many of them as possible in all of your journaling.

SIGHT: beautiful, stunning, gorgeous, adorable, cute, eye-catching, colorful, rich, vivid, vibrant, lively, artistic, handsome, good-looking, attractive, tall, soaring, large, giant, small, tiny, petite, miniature, miniscule, ugly, horrible, dreadful, unpleasant, alive, thriving, flourishing, blooming, round, spherical, curved, globular, square, angular, unique, distinctive, rare, unusual, bright, dazzling, brilliant, dark, dim, shady, shadowy, gloomy, sunny, cloudy, clear, picturesque, scenic, pleasing

TOUCH: soft, silky, supple, velvety, squishy, soggy, spongy, smooth, sleek, glossy, wet, damp, soaked, drenched, sopping, dry, parched, dried-out, hard, firm, solid, stiff, rigid, scratchy, rough, abrasive, irritating, coarse, bumpy, irregular, jagged, hot, scorching, boiling, sizzling, sweltering, cold, chilling, freezing, frosty, bitter, arctic, warm, humid, lukewarm, balmy, tickly, painful, sore, tender, aching, raw, throbbing, electrifying, stimulating, moving, thrilling

TASTE: delicious, tasty, appetizing, scrumptious, yummy, luscious, delectable, mouth-watering, salty, savory, spicy, flavorful, aromatic, sweet, sugary, syrupy, dry, moist, tender, tough, sour, tart, bitter, vinegary, disgusting, sickening, horrible, repulsive, yucky, rotten, putrid, fresh, crisp, juicy, garden-fresh, ice-cold, refreshing, bubbly

SOUND: music, tune, harmony, composition, song, sound, resonance, hum, echo, thud, crash, jingle, swish, clatter, clang, ring, bang, hiss, whoosh, whistle, whisper, rustle, yell, shout, scream, shriek, roar, bellow, bawl, cry, screech, howl, holler, laugh, giggle, chuckle, hoot, snort, snicker, cackle, sing, snore, sigh, speak

SMELL: fragrant, perfumed, aromatic, scented, sweet-smelling, flowery, fresh, airy, clean, breezy, refreshing, unpolluted, delicious, tasty, appetizing, scrumptious, yummy, pungent, strong, odorous, musty, stale, rank, stuffy, smelly, stinking, reeking, foul, putrid, yucky, sexy, attractive, organic, natural, woodsy, musky, dirty, sweaty, old, new, new-car, chemical, synthetic, plastic, metallic, wet-dog, burning, smoky

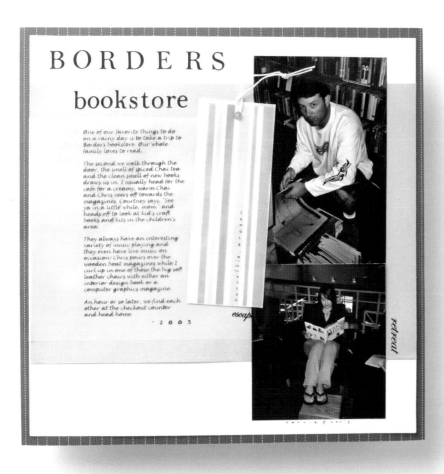

Borders

by Carrie Utley

1. **SUPPLIES:** Patterned Paper: Great Room: Great Little Stripe, Gallery: Chocolate Pinstripe; Cardstock: Dark Olive; Address Stickers: Black; Nails: Olive Round; Other: White Cardstock: Unknown; White Vellum: Unknown

2. **TIP:** Create a simple embellishment by encasing an accent pattern in a handmade vellum envelope. I punched a hole in the end of the envelope, tied a string to it, and added some extra journaling along the lines of the stripe. Don't be afraid to keep your layouts streamlined in order to focus on the photos and journaling. The simplicity of this layout style made it easy for me to think about the moment and what I wanted to capture about it.

3. **MAKE IT MEANINGFUL:** I wanted to take my journaling a little farther than "This is our favorite bookstore". I thought about why we like to go there and what it smells, sounds, tastes, and feels like when we walk in the door. As soon as I could imagine a smell, I thought of the Chai Tea that I love to get there. Then I thought about what I could touch and feel and it made me think of those big comfy leather chairs that I love to sit in while I look at the books. As I started to write and imagine, before I knew it, I was done.

The Joy of Eating

by Mellette Berezoski

1. **SUPPLIES:** Patterned Paper: Rec Room: Denim Stars, Rec Blocks, Den: Dark Den Circles; Cardstock: Light Butter; Tacks: Scarlet, Denim Round; I.D. Tags: Denim and Scarlet; Address Stickers: Denim and Scarlet; Other: label maker tape by Dymo, embossing powder by Suze Weinberg, hemp by Crafts Etc., chalk by Craft T Products, stamping ink by Clearsnap; Fonts: CK Newsprint by Creating Keepsakes and 2Peas Jack Frost downloaded from twopeasinabucket.com

2. **TIP:** Create a cracked glass look on the tags by embossing with UTEE (ultra thick embossing powder) and then cracking when dry.

3. **MAKE IT MEANINGFUL:** My two year old son truly enjoys eating. He seems to think about it all day long. I wanted to document how pleasurable and important it was to him, so I wrote about how it affected all five of his senses.

The Sounds of the Newborn

by Ann-Marie Weis

1. **SUPPLIES:** Patterned Paper: Sitting room: Sitting Flowers, Small Sitting Plaid; Cardstock: Light butter, Dark denim; Tacks: Olive Square; Molding: Butter; Other: olive fluid chalk ink by Colorbox, transparency film by OfficeMax, beads by Modern Romance, silk and lace ribbon (source unknown)

2. **TIP:** I put ink on the silk ribbon to match the patterned paper and wove it through the molding. I printed part of the title on a transparency and attached it to the photo with tacks.

3. **MAKE IT MEANINGFUL:** While we often write about our babies, we often forget to write about the sounds they make. I wanted to evoke some of the sounds you hear the most during the newborn period, like screams, and make a point about how quickly we forget this important part of both our lives.

Our Little Girl

By Jlyne Hanback

1. **SUPPLIES:** Patterned Paper: Butter Bouquet, Spruce Plaid; Cardstock: Dark Butter; I.D. Tags: Spruce; Tacks: Spruce Round; Font: Chatterbox Heber; Scrapbook Windows; Other: Ribbon: Offray; Silk Flowers: Hobby Lobby, Machine Stitching

2. **TIP:** Add femininity to the layout by attaching silk flowers and ribbon in coordinating colors. The silk flowers are attached with tacks. The ribbon is used to attach the I.D. Tags and adds a softness.

3. **MAKE IT MEANINGFUL:** The journaling was written as a letter to my daughter to express to her how important she is to her father and me. I hope that by looking at this page, my daughter will be able to read our feelings about her for years to come, as though we were speaking directly to her. Even after we are long gone, the journaling in a letter format will be a reminder to her of how special she is, directly from our hearts.

My Vivid Autumn

by Melanie Bauer

1. **SUPPLIES:** Patterned Paper: Reading Room: Holiday Plaid; Cardstock: Burgundy; Tacks: Antique Bronze Round; Molding: Olive; Rivet: Antique Bronze; Address Stickers: Burgundy; Other: Pen by Zig Millennium

2. **TIP:** Rotate an alphabet sticker in your title to help catch the eye of those looking at your layout.

3. **MAKE IT MEANINGFUL:** I've never been much of an autumn person, but recently, I became aware of all the beauty that it had to offer. By using the five senses as a jumping point, I was able to more descriptively detail the story behind my photos.

Fall Day

by Kristi Baumgarten

1. **SUPPLIES:** Patterned Paper: Cabin: Olive Stripes, Cabin Plaid, Billiard Room: Billiard Table; Rivets: Antique Bronze; Molding: Olive (sanded, walnut inked, and chalked with Fresco Amaretto Truffle liquid chalk); Other: slide holder with Fresco liquid chalk (Amaretto Truffle), Dymo label maker, Bazzill cardstock for title (inked with the liquid chalk), jute laced through the molding. Fonts: 2Ps Jack Frost (title), 2Ps Chestnuts and Dymo (journaling)

2. **TIP:** Sand and ink the paper for an aged look, thread jute/twine through the molding.

3. **MAKE IT MEANINGFUL:** Fall is my favorite season of the year. There is nothing better than just taking it all in and watching my children experience this wonderful time of year.

Imagine
by Jayla Campbell

1. **SUPPLIES:** Patterned Paper: Gallery: Dark Gallery Swirl, Reading Room: Reading Flowers; Cardstock: Dark Spruce; Tacks: Black Round; Frames: Den; Rivets: White; Address Stickers: White; Other: White Mesh, Green Ribbon: Offray, Stamps-Hero Arts

2. **TIP:** Scrapbook your children's reactions to changes in seasons.

3. **MAKE IT MEANINGFUL:** This was such a fun day. It was Cole's first experience with snow. He was just old enough to wonder what this white stuff was all about. He sat by the window and watched in awe. When he finally got all bundled up, I took him out to explore. He was having the time of his life until he realized the snow was cold.

Silver Lake
by Brooke Campbell

1. **SUPPLIES:** Patterned Paper: Den: Dark Den Circles; Nails: Denim Round; Other: Blue Bazzill, jute, washers, Comic Sans MS font, and ColorBox Amber Clay fluid chalk inkpad

2. **TIP:** Raid your husband's toolbox to find washers or other fun objects.

3. **MAKE IT MEANINGFUL:** My husband and I love to go up in the canyon. We love the mountain air, the beautiful scenery, and everything else that stimulates our five senses.

Disgusting

by Jayla Campbell

1. **SUPPLIES:** Patterned Paper: Sun Room: Sun Room Stripe, Pool Tile; Cardstock: Light Scarlet, Dark Tangerine; Rivets: Tangerine; Scrapbook Addresses: White; Other: White Bazzil, White Ribbon (inked)

2. **TIP:** Use address stickers to describe the thoughts and feelings…word by word!

3. **MAKE IT MEANINGFUL:** I will never forget this moment. It was the day I saw my son's true personality shine through– determined and strong willed. He was sure to let me know that there was no way he was going to eat this stuff!

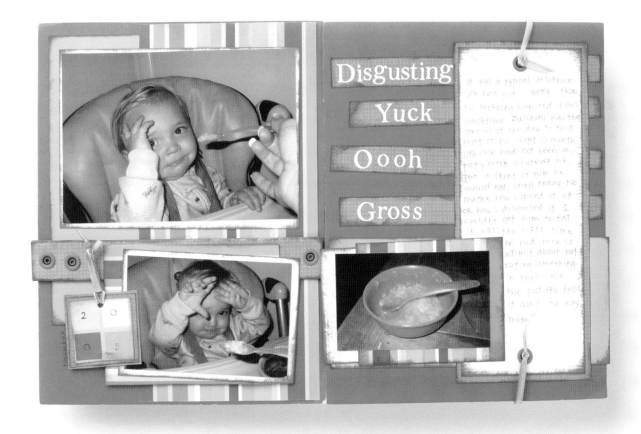

INTERVIEWING

INTERVIEWING

Who is a hero to you from the past? Abraham Lincoln? Mother Teresa? How do we know about the heroic way that they lived their lives, even though they died a long time ago? Someone took the time to interview and write about these people so that, generations later, their stories would still inspire and uplift. It is almost certain there's a heroic person in your life whose story has never been told.

Sure, you can scrapbook about someone without interviewing them, but think about the remarkable material you would have if you took the time to really delve into their feelings, and let their own words be your journaling. Often in interviews, you'll find out things that you never would have guessed to be true, and you'll be so thankful that you chose to ask, instead of assume what the answers would be.

Interviewing works especially well for pages and albums about parents and grandparents, because they lived so much of their lives before you were ever born. Interviewing is also extremely effective for mentors, teachers, or heroes in your life. Interviewing the spouse or close loved ones of someone who has passed away is a noble way of making a tribute to someone you never got the chance to interview, but would have liked to.

In fact, interviewing can work for anyone you are interested in learning more about, or feel compelled to scrapbook about. Children are exceptionally fun to interview, because you never know what will come out of their little mouths.

To interview, simply write down every question you can think to ask. Think about everything that you wish you knew, and think about things that you think you know, but would like to verify. You can do a lifetime interview, or you can interview someone about a specific topic or event in his or her life (i.e. Military service, current events, career).

Once you have the questions organized, coordinate a time to meet. Make sure you are able to have uninterrupted time together in a quiet place. Turn off your phone and let the person you are interviewing know that you value their time, and you are giving them 100% of your listening ears. It's a good idea to take a voice recorder or video camera along so you can make an accurate account of his/her answers.

If you cannot meet with this person directly, you can also mail or email him/her the questions and have the sheet returned to you with the questions answered.

Here are some sample questions to ask when interviewing:

How did you get to where you are today?
What is your best advice on family, career and personal achievement?
What do you see as your greatest accomplishment?
What were your biggest failures and how did you overcome them?
How have you changed through the years?
What would you still like to accomplish in your lifetime?

Who's Your Daddy?

by Candi Gershon

1. **SUPPLIES:** Patterned Paper: Great Room: Great Big Stripes; Great Little Stripes; Cardstock: Scarlet; Tacks: Antique Gold Round; Rivets: Antique Gold; Other: Jute, Mosaic Letter Tiles, Ink by Colorbox; Fonts: Times New Roman, Toxica, 2Peas Jack Frost

2. **TIP:** Try matting your journaling box with a very thin layer of patterned paper. It will add just the right "pop" without distracting from your text.

3. **MAKE IT MEANINGFUL:** I interviewed my husband, so one day my kids may know him a little better. I asked him ten questions about everything from his first car to how he first knew he loved me. I also included pictures along the bottom of the layout that relate to some of his answers.

Proud of her

by Jayla Campbell

1. **SUPPLIES:** Patterned Paper: Sitting: Small Sitting Plaid, Light Sitting Stripe; Love Tiles: My Mother; Tacks: Black Round; Other: Brown Cardstock, Ribbon

2. **TIP:** Use the Love Tiles to inspire yourself on what to interview someone else about.

3. **MAKE IT MEANINGFUL:** Cody has so much love and respect for his mother. This is something I saw in him before we were even married. He absolutely loved this picture taken candidly on our wedding day. I wanted to have him share why he is so proud of her.

What makes me proud of him

by Jayla Campbell

1. **SUPPLIES:** Patterned Paper: Sun Room: Pool Tile; Cardstock: Dark Tangerine, Dark Sand; I.D. Tags: Denim; Love Tiles: My Son; Frames: Den; Tacks: Round Denim; Other: Fibers (unknown)

2. **TIP:** Add tacks to create a different element to the patterned paper

3. **MAKE IT MEANINGFUL:** It is obvious to all who meet my mother-in-law that she is so proud of every one of her 13 children. Her eyes light up whenever she speaks about any of them. I asked her to tell me why she was proud of Cody and this is what she said.

Confessions Of A Teenager

by Vanessa Reyes

1. **SUPPLIES:** Patterned Paper: Great Room: Great Little Plaid, Scarlet Bloom; Cardstock: Light Scarlet, Light Butter, Light Spruce; Address Stickers: Black; Rivets: Olive; Tacks: Bronze Square; Nails: Butter; Frames: Billard; Love Tiles: My pet; Molding: Scarlet; I.D. Tags: Denim; Other: metal rim tags: Making Memories; wire hands: The Card Connection; letter stamps: Ma Vinci and Hero Arts; Other: fabric, office tags, and mesh.

2. **TIP:** Capturing a stage or a milestone through the journey of life can be one of our most prized memories. As we get older, we tend to take pride, or sometimes poke fun, at our growing personalities and mistakes. Make it an easy journey by dedicating a layout just to these moments in time.

3. **MAKE IT MEANINGFUL:** I wanted to celebrate the beauties as well as the trials of being a teenager. By interviewing my 13 year old cousin Leilani, I received a first hand look at teenagers in this generation. I know this special layout will be one to treasure and look back on often.

My mother has always told me "If I could have done it all over again I would have had ten more kids." She always said that family is all you get to take with you when you leave this life. Mom and dad have touched our lives in so many ways we could never repay them. I asked each of my brothers and sisters what the most memorable lesson was that they have learned from mom and dad. This is their legacy.

The Guys

by Brooke Campbell

1. **SUPPLIES:** Patterned Paper: Den: Light Den Stripe; Cardstock: Light Spruce Solid, Dark Denim Solid; Frames: Den; Other: white Bazzill, black chalk, and Typist font

2. **TIP:** Your journaling does not have to be too complicated. Just write something simple.

3. **MAKE IT MEANINGFUL:** I tried to interview the guys for this page. They obviously thought they were too cool for that, so I wrote that down.

A Day At the Zoo

by Jessi Stringham

1. **SUPPLIES:** Patterned Paper: Den: Light Den Stripe, Den Weave, Light Den Blocks (reverse side used for journaling); Cardstock: Dark Denim Solid, Dark Spruce (Bazzill); Address Stickers: Denim Chippy Circles; Tacks: Spruce and Denim; Rub-ons: Chippy Black (discover), Emotion (content), Travel (uncharted territory); Buttons: Chatterbox Buttons by Junkitz (Den and Cabin); Other: Fonts: Century Gothic; Ink: Ranger Industries– Distress Ink

2. **TIP:** I had a lot of journaling on this layout, so I decided to create a file folder tab out of my journaling and tuck it under the pictures. I had so many pictures from that day, and it was hard to pick just three! I used the tacks and the rub-ons to highlight three key words to describe the day.

3. **MAKE IT MEANINGFUL:** It was definitely fun to interview my husband about his thoughts on our first visit to the zoo with our son, Jaden. I usually do most of the journaling on my layouts, but it's nice for him to add his own thoughts from time to time. Of course that means there will be a lot of sarcasm and his silly personality, but that's what I love about it. It's especially fun to see his point of view and excitement over a simple visit to the zoo.

Our Little Girl

by Kari Barrera

1. **SUPPLIES:** Patterned Paper: Den: Denim Weave, Light Den Stripe, Powder room: Rosie Posie, Sitting Room: Sitting Room Flowers; Love: Powder Room; Tacks: Rosey Square; Other: buttons, silk flowers, toile, textured ribbon, metal chain link

2. **TIP:** Alter the color or texture of the paper by adding paint and crinkling it.

3. **MAKE IT MEANINGFUL:** In an effort to record how the family feels about our new daughter, I decided to go around the house and ask each member to tell me a few things they loved about her. Then I simply listed them and attached them to the layout. To add some fun, I wrote who said what on each strip of paper.

Who Knew?

by Christy Tomlinson

1. **SUPPLIES:** Patterned Paper: Rec Room: Rec Room Blocks, Rec Room Weave; Cardstock: Dark Denim; Tacks: Round Silver; Font: Chatterbox Rust; Other: Ink: Tim Holtz Distressed Ink by Rangers- Vintage Photo; Buttons: Junkits Chatterbox Series- Rec Room; Corrugated Paper

2. **TIP:** I used a series of pictures to show my son's personality. I wanted this layout to reflect him. I used word strips to ask questions I didn't know about it, and larger words strips for him to write on for the answers.

3. **MAKE IT MEANINGFUL:** It's funny, but sometimes I don't think I know anything about my children. Braden and I were traveling in the car on a road trip back to our hometown. He had a bag of Skittles he was munching on. After I asked him if I could have some, I started to dig out only the red ones (my favorite). I stopped myself and realized I was probably taking his favorite color too. Just to be sure, I asked him what his favorite Skittle was. He told me lemon! I couldn't believe it! LEMON? I don't know anyone whose favorite Skittle was lemon! Well it made me wonder what else I didn't know about him, so this layout was inspired by that conversation. I wrote down the questions I wanted to know about him, and he wrote the answers on a piece of paper for me. I used his actual handwriting for this page because I wanted it to be more personal.

First Date
January 1990

I have this policy, I only date the same guy twice.

Yeh, I understand. I have a girlfriend, we're just taking a break and dating other people for a while.

That's great! We can just hang-out and have fun!

Yeh, I'll honestly probably end up marrying her someday.

Wow! I'm not getting married until I'm 30! I'm going to go to art school, move to the city and start a design firm. Then, maybe I'll have 2 kids at the most.

That's cool, do you want to go hang out tomorrow? Oh yeh, and there's this party next week, wanna go?

Six weeks later
March 1990

I think I'm really in love with you. And, I'm ready to really move on with life. I know you're not ready for what I want...so this is really hard. We should probably just stop seeing each other.

If you asked me to marry you, I'd probably say yes.

...choke.

Eleven years later
October 2001

Happy Birthday, Babe, can I get you something? I'm sorry you're in the hospital on your 30th birthday.

I just want to see the baby. I am in a lot of pain...I'm so glad we're both o.k.

I know, we almost lost you both.

Can you believe we have 5 kids!?

Yeh, I can. I love our life.

Me, too.

TIMELINES

TIMELINES

It's always remarkable to watch something transform from start to finish. I think we all have the desire to see things grow, change and improve. Creating a timeline helps to form a sense of 'being there' during the different stages of lifetime progression.

Think of parts of your life that have had particular points that were extremely pivotal and meaningful to you. Begin by writing the dates and particulars of these stages or events. When you have chronologically ordered these events, try to find photos to correspond with them. If you don't have photos for all of them, don't let that stop you...maybe you can just find an illustrative icon or simply title that stage in your timeline.

There are a lot of possibilities for timelines, here are some ideas to have a go at:

• Locate photos of yourself with different hair and fashion styles dating back as far as you can; make a timeline, complete with dates, of your changing hair and clothing styles. Write about which were your favorites and least favorites and why.

• Find or take photos of all of the homes you have lived in. Make a dated timeline and write what you remember about each home.

• Think about your favorite hobby, when you started and how deeply involved you are in it now. Make a timeline of different phases of skill,

involvement, etc. Write about how this hobby has enhanced your life.

• Make a timeline of the different stages of your marriage or special relationship, from the time you dreamed about the kind of person you wanted to be with, to the time you met, to your first home, to now.

• Think about the different cars you have owned, or different modes of transportation you have used. Make a timeline of the way you got to school, to college, your first car, what you drove in between what you drive now, etc.

• Create a timeline of the years you have known your best friend, from when you met, to trips or experiences you have had together, to now. Write about what this person has meant to you through the years.

• Think about the different 'families' you have been a part of over the years, and who you have lived with. Gather photos of yourself with your parents and siblings, then photos with your roommates; then photos of starting out with your spouse, then with your children. Write about how your life has changed because of the people you have lived with.

• Ponder about how your values have changed and how you have changed as a person. Make a timeline of your educational, spiritual, and personal progression. Chart what the most important things were to you at different times in your life.

Caution: Fragile

by Robin Hohenstern

1. **SUPPLIES:** Patterned Paper: Cabin: Burgundy daisy; Cardstock: Dark Burgundy; Molding: Fawn; I.D. Tags: Burgundy; Tacks: Antique Gold; Other: Walnut Ink; Stencil: Plaid; Black Acrylic Paint: Plaid; Marker: Sharpie; 1" gauze; cardboard; Brown Ink: Nick Bantock/Ranger; Sand paper (for sanding picture)

2. **TIP:** If you make a mistake on the hand journaling on the I.D. Tag, just put some other cardstock on top and try again!

3. **MAKE IT MEANINGFUL:** My poor little girl always seems to have everything "bad" happen to her. I wanted to document her injuries/major events on this layout.

Love, Honor, Trust

by Jayla Campbell

1. **SUPPLIES:** Patterned Paper: Sitting room: Sitting flowers; Frames: Den; Nails: Frosty Clear, Other: ribbon: Offray; clear vellum; Fonts: Wendy Medium, Palace Script

2. **TIP:** Add different elements to the frames by covering the text with flowers, etc.

3. **MAKE IT MEANINGFUL:** I want to be able to vividly remember this day for as long as I live.

My Story

by Christy Tomlinson

1. **SUPPLIES:** Patterned Paper: Gallery: Light Gallery Blossoms; Cardstock: Light Rosey; Rivets: Taupe; Other: Photo Corner: White (unknown); Sewing Machine Decorative Stitch; Ink: Tim Holtz Distressed Ink by Ranger- Vintage Photo; Ribbon: Offray, Dymo Lable Maker

2. **TIP:** I used the photo corners to tie the pictures all together and keep them uniform. I also used my sewing machine and a decorative stitch to add depth to the layout.

3. **MAKE IT MEANINGFUL:** When I was in labor with my 4th child I suffered from a stroke. It was one of the most terrifying experiences of my life. My doctor told me strokes were often common in obese women during pregnancy. I was shocked! I had never considered myself obese! I knew I had gained a lot of weight over the last five years, but I hadn't realized I was now nearly 100 pounds overweight. I found out a few months later I had a disease called PCO, which if not monitored would cause cancer and I would never be able to have children again. I knew I wanted more children, so I had to do something. One thing that would help conquer my disease was to loose the weight I had put on. It seemed impossible but my doctor assured me I could do it. It was a long process, but by eating right and exercising more, within nine months I had lost almost 90 pounds. It was one of the hardest things I had ever done, but it was well worth it. Three months after I lost the weight I found out I was pregnant with my fifth child, Ethan. I am so grateful for him and am glad for the personal journey it took to get him here. Two years later I find myself expecting our sixth child and I am so grateful for the opportunity I have to bring another child into our precious family. I can't think of a more rewarding end to my story. Doing something for yourself isn't always selfish, it is giving to those who love you as well.

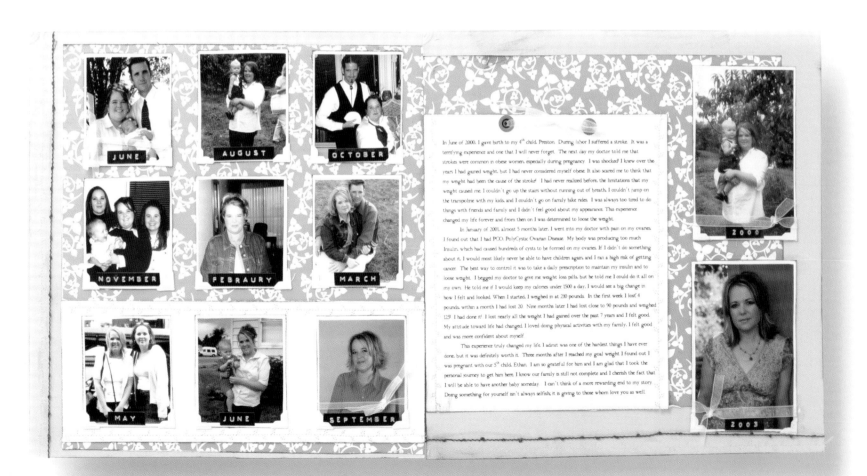

JoAnn

by Carrie Utley

1. **SUPPLIES:** Patterned Paper: Great Room: Butter Bloom, Butter & Olive Stripe; Cardstock: Light Olive; I.D. Tags: Olive; Addresses Stickers: Black; Other: Ribbon: Offray; Mini Jewelry Tags: Viking Office Supply

2. **TIP:** In order to include a sample of my mother's handwriting, I asked her to jot down a few notes about each photo. I rolled up the original note, tied it with a ribbon, and glued the ribbon to the layout.

3. **MAKE IT MEANINGFUL:** My mother had a stack of old photos of herself and her life before we came into the picture. I had looked through them on many occasions, noting the cheap price of Hamburgers (25 cents!) and the little Volkswagon that I had heard so much about. I knew the stories behind these photos were many, and I felt intimidated by the task of "where to start". I decided to start with a title layout and a table of contents of sorts. I numbered each photo and asked my mom to tell me just one or two things about each one. Now, I have a starting place. I can begin a new layout or page about photo number one, and ask my mom to tell me all about the young lady in the photo (my mom) with those funky curlers in her hair.

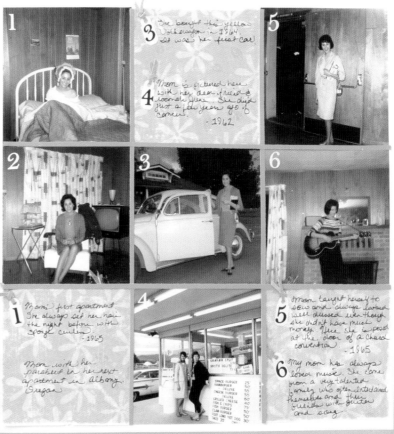

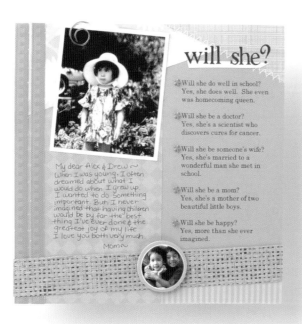

Will She?

by Leah Fung

1. **SUPPLIES:** Patterned Papers: Reading Room: Spruce Gerbers, Den: Den Stripe; Tacks: Antique Silver Flower; Address Stickers: Black; I.D. Tags: Spruce; Molding; Fawn; Other: Italian paper clip, weaved mat; Times New Roman font

2. **TIP:** Try I.D. Tags for a quick mini photo mat. Mount on foam tape for added dimension.

3. **MAKE IT MEANINGFUL:** For a different twist on a timeline, ask simple chronological questions.

Eleven Years Later

by Melody Ross

1. **SUPPLIES:** Patterned Papers: Gallery: Black Gallery Blossoms, Dark Gallery Swirl, Chocolate Gallery Swirl, Gallery Skinny Stripe; Frames: Gallery; Other: White Tacks; Ribbon; Offray, Font: Houston's Pen and Myriad

2. **TIP:** Create an envelope out of coordinating paper to put special love letters inside.

3. **MAKE IT MEANINGFUL:** It's amazing how much we thought we knew as teenagers. I was certain that I did not want to marry or have children until I was at least 30. My life took a different road than what I planned as a teenager. Instead of marrying when I was 30, I was celebrating the birth of my fifth child after 12 years of marriage!

Boy meets Girl

by Jayla Campbell

1. **SUPPLIES:** Patterned Paper: Great Room: Scarlet Bloom, Great Room Stripe; Cardstock: Dark Burgundy, Dark Spruce, Light Sand; I.D. Tags: Scarlet; Tacks: Antique Bronze Round; Other: White Mesh, Hemp Cord, Wooden Letters; Font: CK Gutenberg

2. **TIP:** Documenting two people's perspectives of the same timeline can be very different. For example, my husband and I have a completely different story of how things happened from the time we met to the day of our wedding.

3. **MAKE IT MEANINGFUL:** I did this book for my husband as a Christmas gift. We had always said we needed to write down our story before we started to forget the details. The only catch was that he had to finish it by adding his side of the story.

Who: My adventurous thrill seeking husband

What: RockcLimBing

When: Whenever he can. He'll even sneak out of work a little early just to head up the canyon to _____ climb before coming home.

Where: Any rock big enough to climb. He loves to climb in the Wasatch Mountains not far from our home. Whenever we go to Idaho to visit family he loves the opportunity to drive through to the City of Rocks.

Why: Cody has a love and a passion for rockclimbing. He loves being outdoors and being active. The challenge is thrilling for him.

who, what, when,
WHERE, WHY

who, what, when,
WHERE, WHY

Sure, these are the basics! But, let's admit it, it's always the basic things that end up being the most important when all is said and done.

I try to keep in mind a trunk of priceless, nameless photographs at my grandmother's house. Early in my marriage, I had every intention of going to her house to help her label these historic pieces of my heritage. At least half of the photos came from my grandfather's side of the family, and there were photos that were nearly 100 years old. I was certain, as I still am now, each of those photos had a story begging to be told and written down. My grandfather died weeks after he was diagnosed with cancer, and once he was gone, the stories in those photos were lost forever. I missed a chance I can never, ever get back.

This is not a unique story, but the fact this happens so often does not make it any less heartbreaking. I know there are photos in closets and in boxes all over the world that will end up in garage sales. It is tragic when anyone who could have told the stories in old photos has passed away, and no one took the time to write them down.

This certainly is a reason to write down the basic information of who, what, when, where and why!

Beyond that, it is also a really fun and easy way to journal! You can take one simple photograph and really dig a lot of meaning out of it if you answer these five straightforward questions!

Look at the photos hanging on your wall and piled in your shoeboxes and ask yourself if you have even written down the five basics for them. Imagine if something tragic happened to your family and the simple, basic, most important facts of your life had never been written down. Just because you know who each person is in your photos, that certainly gives no certainty others will know.

Someday, your children will want to know who your friends were, what you did when you spent time together, when you got together, where you got together, and why that friendship was important to you.

In the future, you'll be glad you took the time to document who you worked with, what you worked on, when you worked, where you worked and why you spent time working.

Certainly, it will be meaningful to your posterity to know WHO their family was, what they stood for, when they were born, when they married, where they lived and why they made the decisions they made.

Make it fun, make it boring, make it humorous or very true-life and serious…as long as the facts are straight, you're doing a terrific and very important job.

Side by Side

by Dana Smith

1. **SUPPLIES:** Patterned Paper: Billiard Room: Billiard Stripe; Address Stickers: Denim Chippy, Other: shoe lace, Dymo label maker, jumbo clip: Office Depot

2. **TIP:** I took apart the jumbo clip and used half of it. By attaching it to the top of my journaling sheet I mimicked the look of a clip board. Instead of using ribbon I wrapped a shoe lace around the layout and tied it with a bow.

3. **MAKE IT MEANINGFUL:** For the past four years I have run every week day morning with the same three women. I decided to do a scrapbook page about our running group. One of my friends just had a baby so she had not been able to run with us, but I wanted to some how include her in my page. By taking photos of her in her running shoes while holding her new baby, I think I was able to do just that.

A-MAZE-ing Gift

by Jlyne Hanback

1. **SUPPLIES:** Patterned Paper: Rec Room: Scarlet Butter Stripe, Scarlet Dots; Cardstock: Dark Scarlet, Dark Spruce, Dark Butter; Frames: Rec Room; Rivets: Scarlet; Molding: Spruce, Rub-Ons: Rust; Other: Fabric: Hobby Lobby, Machine Stitching

2. **TIP:** Include all of the important facts about an event by using hand-journaled tags that tell Who, What, When, Where, and Why.

3. **MAKE IT MEANINGFUL:** The photos in this layout tell a story, but I wanted to ensure that the important details were also remembered. I created individual tags with handwritten journaling to give the viewer all of the information needed in order to follow the story. I took a close-up shot of the gift for added effect.

Evidence
by Vanessa Reyes

1. **SUPPLIES:** Patterned Paper: Billiard Room: Billiard Circles, Reading Room: Spruce & Taupe Stripe; Cardstock: Light Butter, Dark Scarlet; I.D. Tags: Scarlet; Rivets: Butter; Tacks: Bronze Star and Square, Address Stickers: Black and Scarlet; Other: Paint: Delta; Stamps: Ma Vinci and Hero Arts; Cork; Fabric

2. **TIP:** Using a transparency sheet can give you the great look of a window or vellum. Try using it in the place of patterned paper, or your title. Also try adding some paint for a glass-like look.

3. **MAKE IT MEANINGFUL:** Who knew bashing a beaten up car could be such fun! A local fair gave us the opportunity to just that. It was a great way to get out some built up aggressions and stress.

Bubble Science
by Kari Barrera

1. **SUPPLIES:** Patterned Paper: Den: Light Den Stripe, Big Den Stripe, Cardstock: Light Denim; Address Stickers: Denim; I.D. Tags: Olive; Rivets: Cream; Other: raffia, denim fabric, silk flower, chalk, acrylic paint

2. **TIP:** Brush a light wash of white acrylic paint across your patterned paper.

3. **MAKE IT MEANINGFUL:** Using the "Five W's" to help me recall all the details of this fun experiment day, I was able to record things like the cold morning, and how Mr. Rogers was the catapult for the whole idea. I love recording the fun elements that home-schooling has brought to our family. It seems everything we do somehow turns into a wonderful learning experience.

Brett and Coltyn

by Jayla Campbell

1. **SUPPLIES:** Patterned Paper: Den: Den Blocks, Cardstock: Dark Denim, Light Sand; Frames: Den; Tacks: Denim Round, Address Stickers: Butter; Other: Ribbon

2. **TIP:** When journaling a "who, when, why, what, where", add a different element to the topics to make them stand out on your page.

3. **MAKE IT MEANINGFUL:** My nephews, Brett and Coltyn, mean the world to me. Since I have been married and had a child of my own, I don't get to spend as much time with them as I used to. It meant so much to me when they came to visit me this last year. We had so much fun. I realized they weren't the little boys I used to know. They have grown up to be very respectable young men.

Rockclimbing

by Jayla Campbell

1. **SUPPLIES:** Patterned Paper: Great Room: Dark Chocolate Stripe, Den Room: Big Den Plaid; Rivets: Antique Bronze; Address Stickers: Black & Black Chippy Circles; Other: Black Cardstock, Brown Cardstock, Hemp Cord, Wood Frame, Rocks

2. **TIP:** Scrapbook someone else's hobby and ask them the who, what, when, why, and where.

3. **MAKE IT MEANINGFUL:** My Husband Cody spends the majority of his summer rock climbing. It is something he loves to do. Adding this page to my scrapbook will show our children his love for this sport and why.

Saving Halloween

by Carrie Utley

1. **SUPPLIES:** Patterned Paper: Cabin: Olive Daisy, Olive Plaid, Olive Daisy Vellum; Cardstock: Dark Olive; Windows: Round; Foundations: Cream; Other: Ribbon: Offray; White Pen: Galaxy Marker; White Vellum: Unknown

2. **TIP:** Make it easy to journal by doing it in stages. I printed out several sentences about things that happened that night onto vellum. I glued several strips to the title page and attached the longer ones over my photos on the second page.

3. **MAKE IT MEANINGFUL:** When I developed the photos from our first Halloween in our new home, some of the film had been damaged leaving me with only a few photos of just my daughter. Although my daughter makes a nice subject for this layout, I still wanted to remember the entire event and the other people who were there, even without the pictures. I jotted down a comment from each family member and recorded it onto a tag with their name on it. Then I tied all the tags together and placed them into a pocket created by one of the photos. Now, all I have to do is pull out the bundle of tags to remember the evening with my family.

Big Girl Bangs

by Christy Tomlinson

1. **SUPPLIES:** Patterned Paper: Parlor: Soft Olive Stems, Parlor Tablecloth, and Violet Stems; Cardstock: Light Olive (Bazzill); Rub-ons: Chippy Black and Typewriter Black; Tags: Parlor stitched tags and Violet ID tags; Other: Ink: TimHolz Vintage Photo by Ranger; Flower: Prima; Ribbon and small white tags: Making Memories; Font: Emmascript downloaded from the Internet

2. **TIP:** Chatterbox Rub-ons are great for use on any size tag. They are perfect for journaling, quotes are even words. I love using them for Tittles as well.

3. **MAKE IT MEANINGFUL:** Ever since Allie was a little girl, she has cut her own hair at LEAST eight or more times. The last time she cut her hair, I told her if she ever did it again, I would shave her head bald! All of Allie's "big girl" friends, had bangs and so she came to me a few weeks later, asking me if could cut her hair so she could look like a big girl! I was so impressed that she didn't just do it herself. It really showed me she truly was a "big" girl now! She loves her bangs and tells everyone she meets how she finally got a BIG girl bangs!

Time well spent

by Melody Ross

1. **SUPPLIES:** Cardstock: Bazzill; Patterned Paper: Sunroom Bias Plaid and Tangerine Gingham; Id Tags: Denim, Tangerine, and Olive; Stitched Tags: Den; Mailboxes: Sunroom; Tacks: Round Olive; Rivets: Tangerine; Photo corners: White; Other: Raffia

2. **TIP:** Use All different styles of Chatterbox tags for your journaling. I used a mailbox to hold a few of the tags I created. These tags pull out and create an interactive layout.

3. **MAKE IT MEANINGFUL:** I cherish the little, everyday moments in life. I love these moments every bit as much as the holidays, vacations, and other big events, maybe even more. I want to look back and remember all of the normal little things that made my life so full of joy. Seeing my husband interacting with our children is definitely one of my favorite little things in life.

letters to OTHERS

letters to OTHERS

I had a close, very important, and irreplaceable friend die tragically when I was 25 years old. I remember the grief and sorrow like it was yesterday and I still feel so many voids from her loss. During the darkest parts of my grieving, I wrote her letters, and I feel that it was an enormous part of my recovering from her loss. Now, I have fresh memories of my relationship and feelings for her that bring her back to my heart within just a few minutes of reading.

Writing a letter is a powerful way to connect with someone that you can't be with and tell them how you feel about them. There are a lot of reasons we can't be with someone. Whether it's because the relationship is estranged, or because they have passed away, or even because they haven't gotten here yet (a future child, or future spouse), we can always express those feelings in a letter.

Letter writing is a wonderful thing to do for people we are close to and talk to every day, as well. It's a great technique to use when you are creating a page or an album for someone, and you know they will soon have it in their hands to read.

I admired the way that Leah Fung wrote a letter to her future grandchildren (see page 96), even though her little boys are barely out of pre-school. I think it's a form of goal setting, and it touched my heart to know that she, too, was already looking forward to being a grandmother someday. I often think of my future grandchildren and plan to write them letters because of Leah's influence.

I am making an album for my husband, as a tribute to our years together, and most of the journaling inside is in the form of a letter to him. I chose this tone because I am making the album just for him. I know that my children and grandchildren will probably read through it someday too, but it will be as if they are reading love letters I wrote to him. I love the thought of that.

You'll be surprised at how easily the words come. Be honest and don't worry about how you sound. Let all of your feelings out as if the person you are writing it to will be able to read the letter.

Just start writing…"Dear _____,"

My Brother

by Jayla Campbell

1. **SUPPLIES:** Patterned Paper: Rec Room: Scarlet & Butter Stripe Vellum, Billiard Room: Billiard Pinstripes; Cardstock: Dark Scarlet; Molding: Scarlet; Love: My Brother, Tacks: Antique Gold Round; Other: Fonts: Wendy Medium, Schindler Small Caps

2. **TIP:** Writing a letter to someone who has passed away helps preserve the memories you still have about him or her.

3. **MAKE IT MEANINGFUL:** We lost my brother Scott 17 years ago to a car accident. I was only nine at the time, but still remember how hard it was. Getting older, I have realized there are many things that I have begun to forget about him. I have written this letter to preserve those memories.

Time Has Flown

by Heather Preckel

1. **SUPPLIES:** Patterned Paper: Parlor Room: Parlor Posies and Parlor Plaid; Cardstock: Light Olive and Light Violet; Rivets: Antique Bronze; Other: gingham ribbon: Ofray, twill: Wrights, clock stamp: Magenta, Memories Black: Stamp Craft, note book paper: Carolina Paper

2. **TIP:** Run twill through printer; crinkle and sand chatterbox paper; ink the edges of notebook paper.

3. **MAKE IT MEANINGFUL:** I have always liked to write notes, and I find it so easy to put my feelings down on paper rather than actually saying them. I want my daughter to know my heart and how much I love her. I want her to know I took the time to sit down and write her a letter that I know she will cherish as she grows older.

My Baby, My Future

by Melanie Bauer

1. **SUPPLIES:** Patterned Paper: Cabin: Burgundy Daisy, Small Cabin Stripe Vellum; Cardstock: Dark Fawn, Burgundy; Nails: Fawn; I.D. Tags: Burgundy; Address Stickers: Fawn and Burgundy; Molding: Fawn; Other: Pen by Zig Millennium; Fiber by unknown; Stamp by Office Depot; Ink by Nick Bantock; Button by Doodlebug.

2. **TIP:** Use molding to direct attention to your title without being too bold or distracting.

3. **MAKE IT MEANINGFUL:** My husband and I talk about our future children's names on an ongoing basis, usually with him nixing all of my ideas. Without writing details like this down, our future children, as well as my husband and I, would likely forget the details of these conversations.

Perfect Love

by Amy Yingling

1. **SUPPLIES:** Patterned Paper: Olive stripes, Olive Daisy Vellum, Dark Den Circles; Cardstock: Dark Sand and Dark Fawn; Tacks: Bronze Flower; Rivets: Bronze; I.D. Tags: Fawn; Address Stickers: Olive

2. **TIP:** Use your label maker to write a letter, sand the strips, and sponge the edges.

3. **MAKE IT MEANINGFUL:** I found this photo and it made me so grateful to be a mom! I just wanted to share those feelings with my boys. I wanted this layout to show my gratitude for the special gift of being a mother.

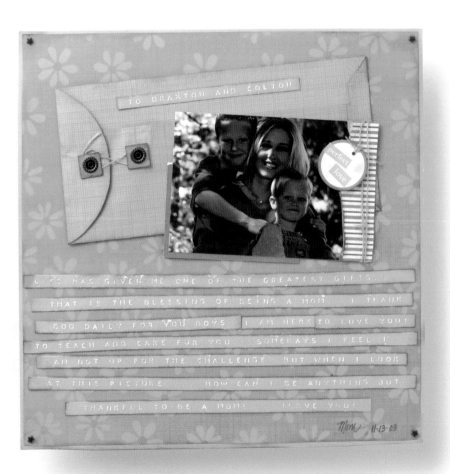

Until We Meet Again

by Tarri Botwinski

1. **SUPPLIES:** Patterned Paper: Cabin: Olive Stripe, Olive Daisy, Cabin Plaid; Cardstock: Cardstock: Light Olive, Light Scarlet; Love: Cabin, Billiard; Molding: Olive; Tacks: Scarlet Flower; Nails: Olive Round; Address Stickers: Black; Other: Amery- MS Word

2. **TIP:** I layered the patterned paper, torn and rolled, and sanded it to give it an aged feel

3. **MAKE IT MEANINGFUL:** There were so many things I never was able to say to my grandmother before she passed on. I know that someday I will be able to tell her, but until then, I wanted to write a letter to her, telling her how much she meant to me and about the things that have happened to me. It was so wonderful to tell her the things I had been holding inside.

Precious Spirits

by Vanessa Reyes

1. **SUPPLIES:** Patterned Papers: Cottage: Butter Bouquet, Powder Room: Rosey Blossoms, Rosey Stripe; I.D. Tags: Rosey; Love Tiles: Our Little Girl- Powder Room; Address Stickers: Fawn; Other: buttons: EK success; ribbons: Europa Imports, Offray; paint: Delta; pins: Li'l Davis Designs; stamps: Ma Vinci, charms: Blue Moon Beads; bead chain and jump rings (unknown).

2. **TIP:** Using fabric can be a creative way to add texture or pattern. Try experimenting with fabric swatches or scraps.

3. **MAKE IT MEANINGFUL:** I love to try to capture a child's spirit expressed in a photograph. The special memory made with a smirk or a smile can be the best memories to remember.

One Day You'll Understand

Kari Barrera

1. **SUPPLIES:** Patterned Paper: Gallery: Light Gallery Blossom, Gallery Bouquet, Light Chocolate Open Dot; Cardstock: Light Rosey; Nails: Black; Other: beads, silk flowers, black ball trim

2. **TIP:** Combining Chatterbox nails with silk flowers can really tie the page together. The Nails also act as a great fastener for the flowers.

3. **MAKE IT MEANINGFUL:** I find that I am always thinking about all the amazing parts of being a mother, and how I look forward to the day when I can express all these feelings to my daughter. I decided to write her a letter to help her to one day better understand this amazing time in my life.

The Man You Have Become

by Dana Smith

1. **SUPPLIES:** Patterned Paper: Sitting Room: Small Sitting Weave, Light Sitting Stripe; I.D. Tags: Taupe; Tacks: Brushed Silver Round; Other: PSX Stamps, Memories Ink, Acrylic Paint and Ribbon (unknown)

2. **TIP:** Paint the I.D. Tags to add emphasis to the titles and main ideas of your layout.

3. **MAKE IT MEANINGFUL:** This photo is of my father and three of his grandchildren. When ever he is around them, he is as happy as any one person can be. It was not always that way. Family has not always been a priority, but I wanted to write about how all that has changed.

Thank You Raeann

by Amy Yingling

1. **SUPPLIES:** Patterned Paper: Parlor: Parlor Posies, Parlor Plum, Parlor Olive; Cardstock: Light Butter; Love Tiles: ThankYou; Tacks: Antique Bronze Flowers.

2. **TIP:** For a softer look print your photos on textured cardstock.

3. **MAKE IT MEANINGFUL:** I never had the chance to say goodbye to a dear friend, but putting my feelings on a page helped give me closure. Create a page as a way to remember a special friendship, and don't be afraid to journal your feelings.

Perfect Love

by Erica Hernandez

1. **SUPPLIES:** Patterned Paper: Gallery: Chocolate Gallery Swirl, Big Gallery Stripe; Address Stickers: Scarlet and Black; Nails: Black Round; I.D. Tag: Black Oval; Molding: Black; Other: Letter Stamps: PSX; Stamping Ink: Colorbox; Ribbon: Unknown; Envelope: Unknown

2. **TIP:** Molding strips make great dividers between different patterned papers. Nails or tacks add dimension and interest to the strips.

3. **MAKE IT MEANINGFUL:** I have so many wishes for my son and his future. I used this layout to document some wishes for his future wife and him to read once he is married.

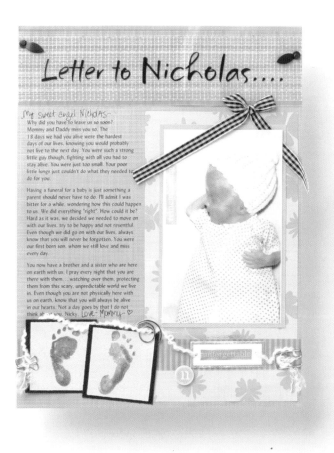

Letter to Nicholas
by Kristi Baumgarten

1. **SUPPLIES:** Patterned Paper: Sitting Room: Sitting Flowers, Small Sitting Plaid, Fawn Stripe Vellum; Cardstock: Light Sand; Address Stickers: Taupe Chippy Circles; I.D. Tag: Taupe; Other: Drywall Mesh; Ribbon; Paper Clips; Button; Fiber; Fonts: McBoo Hallmark, Arial

2. **TIP:** Print title on transparency and layer it over drywall mesh for added texture and dimension.

3. **MAKE IT MEANINGFUL:** It is important to me to scrapbook about everything in my life, not just the happy moments. When we lost our first child, I never thought I would be able to do a scrapbook page about it. Seven years later I am able to journal about my feelings, and it is great therapy to me.

To All My Grandchildren
by Leah Fung

1. **SUPPLIES:** Patterned Paper: Den: Boy Stripe, Rec Room: Denim Stars, Powder Room: Rosey Posey; Rivets: Rosey; Other: Ribbon; Charm; Font: Times New Roman

2. **TIP:** To make roll frames, cut out eight squares of Chatterbox Patterned Paper. Lay each paper on a flat surface. Lay a pencil (or thin rod) along the edge of the paper, then tightly roll the paper around the pencil. Secure the entire seam with small pieces of tape. Roll and secure the other pieces of paper similarly. Using Tombow Mono Multi Liquid glue, glue rolls to a cardstock frame and to each other. If there is any cardstock visible from the front of the frame, trim with scissors.

3. **MAKE IT MEANINGFUL:** Write a letter to your children's children (not yet born), even though it's a loooong way away. It will be something they will always cherish.

Dreams

by Carrie Utley

1. **SUPPLIES:** Patterned Paper: Dark Den Circles, Light Den Circles, Denim Stripe Vellum; Cardstock: Dark Olive; I.D. Tags: Olive; Molding: Olive; Address Stickers: Denim; Nails: Denim Round; Quote for Title: Scrapbookers Best Friend by Chatterbox

2. **TIP:** Create a draped fabric look from your patterned paper for a photo mat. Crumple a paper rectangle, sand it, crumple, and then sand again. It should be very soft and pliable due to the linen content in the paper. Coat the back of the paper with glue stick adhesive and then adhere it to the page while scrunching the paper.

3. **MAKE IT MEANINGFUL:** My husband has always dreamed of building a boat. He reads book after book full of boat building plans, and he has made numerous trips to the Wooden Boat Festival just to be "near" the water and dream. The photo of him looking out onto the water says it all, because it's pretty much the only view I have of him from the moment he hits the water until we head home. In order to relay that feeling in my title, I broke it up into individual words and made two of them stand out..."Dreams" and "Reality".

BEN'S DAD ISN'T KNOWN FOR THE THINGS HE SAYS
BUT RATHER FOR THE LITTLE AND BIG THINGS HE
OFTEN DOES. IT'S ALMOST LIKE HIS SECRET
LANGUAGE. HE SPEAKS THROUGH HIS ACTIONS
RATHER THAN WORDS. DAVE MIGHT NOT VERBALLY
TELL YOU HE LOVES YOU, BUT HE SHOWS YOU
THROUGH PATIENCE, KINDNESS, UNCONDITIONAL
LOVE, AND HARD WORK. HE WOULD GIVE YOU THE
SHIRT OF HIS BACK, THE HOUSE HE LIVES IN, OR EVEN
HIS LIFE SAVINGS IF YOU NEEDED IT. HE'S WILLING TO
GIVE ANYTHING HE HAS TO HELP SOMEONE ELSE.
THAT IS HOW HE SHOWS HIS LOVE. HE'S NOT ALWAYS
A MAN OF MANY WORDS BUT THROUGH HIS OWN
SECRET LANGUAGE HE SPEAKS MUCH
LOUDER THAN ANY WORDS POSSIBLY COULD.

SECRET LANGUAGE

secret LANGUAGES

secret LANGUAGES

What are your secret languages? How do you communicate special things to people in your life in a way that is unique enough to be kept between you?

Secret languages may be words, acts or sounds between two or more people who 'speak the same language'. Think of the different ways you communicate with important people in your life.

Are there hand signs that signal messages? Are there special non-words that speak volumes to you when said by certain people in your life? Are there things that others do for you that communicate much more the act itself?

In my childhood, my brave father would take our entire family of eleven for ice cream nearly every Monday night in our larger-than-life station wagon. We would devour our soft cones and end up in pain with a cold-induced headache. My dad always said "Did you freeze your GOLLY-WHOPPER?" Until I was in high-school, I honestly thought a gollywhopper was a body part. Now my own children gulp down ice cream and cry out "Mom, I froze my gollywhopper!!"

This is a secret language I share with my brothers and sisters, my nieces and nephews, my children...even my husband says it now. It seems as though the giggles and thoughts of these secret little languages unify us in a way that can't be described.

Sometimes secret languages are so secret the recipient doesn't even catch on! My husband has had a quiet policy he would not get dressed for church on Sunday until I was dressed. I never questioned the reasoning for this until one day, I saw him studying my dress closely while he was choosing what tie he would wear with his suit. I didn't let him know I was watching him, but he thoughtfully chose a tie that matched the colors of my dress. I thought about it all through church and asked him about it when we got home. He admitted that, yes, he did want his tie to match my dress so others would always know we go together.

I thought this was about the sweetest thing he'd ever told me, a secret language that may seem a little silly but means the world to me. I think someday, after my husband and I are gone, reading about this act will reveal a lot about the special relationship that we have with each other.

Think carefully about subtle little ways that you communicate, as well as the ways that others communicate to you. Write these things down, you'll never regret the few minutes you sacrificed to help you remember such wonderful parts of your life.

Top Secret

by Amy Yingling

1. **SUPPLIES:** Pattern Pattern: Billiard Room: Billiard Table, Billiard Pinstripes, Billiard Stripes; Cardstock: Dark Fawn; Tacks: Antique Bronze; I.D. Tags: Olive; Other: Van dyke brown stamp pad, Staz-on stamp pad; Stampin'Up! Alphabet stamp; Fonts: CK Typewriter

2. **TIP:** Put letters or words directly onto photos using Staz-on.

3. **MAKE IT MEANINGFUL:** My husband Eli has always liked to give everyone a nickname, so we use secret nicknames around our house. This layout is on how we got them and who gave them to us.

I-J-K-A

by Tarri Botwinski

1. **SUPPLIES:** Patterned Paper: Gallery: Chocolate Gallery Dot, Chocolate Pinstripe; Cardstock: Light Sand; Address Stickers: Black Chippy & Black; Tacks: Antique Bronze Round; Frames: Sitting Room; Other: Font: McGannahan- Internet; Dymo Label Maker; Ink: Close To My Heart

2. **TIP:** I sanded the border of the layout and inked journaling boxes for added texture.

3. **MAKE IT MEANINGFUL:** Every family has little "inside jokes". My son, Jameson, is four and runs around chanting a cheer which makes us all laugh, every time- without fail! I wanted to record this in a layout so we would never forget.

How You Know I Love You

by Melody Ross

1. **SUPPLIES:** Patterned Paper: Great Room: Great Little Stripe, Sitting Room: Fawn Vine; Cardstock: Olive; Rub-ons: Black Typewriter; Other: Photo Corners: White; Font: American Typewriter; Transparency; Ribbon: Naturally Pulsar

2. **TIP:** Create small embellishments with the same Patterned Paper that you use as an accent on the page. Here, a leaf was created out of the same striped paper that is used across the back of the page.

3. **MAKE IT MEANINGFUL:** This is a secret that I don't even think my children know about. I want to make sure that someday they know about all of the little, loving, and thoughtful things that their dad did to be a wonderful husband.

Secret Language

by Christy Tomlinson

1. **SUPPLIES:** Patterned Paper: Sun Room: Cabana Stripe, Tangerine Gingham, and Sun Room Bias Plaid; Cardstock: Light Olive and Light Sky (Bazzill); Rub-ons: Lablemaker Black; Other: Ink: Tim Holtz Distressed Ink by Ranger- Vintage Photo; ribbon and date stamp: Making Memories and May Arts; staples and corrugated paper (unknown); Dymo Label Maker

2. **TIP:** Use colors in your patterned papers that compliment your photos. Sometimes it's intimidating to use patterns with color photos but use small prints and non competing colors to help the pictures remain the focus of the page.

3. **MAKE IT MEANINGFUL:** Ben's dad isn't known for the things he says, but for the things he does. It's almost like his secret language. He speaks through his actions rather than words. I wanted to do a layout that showed secret languages aren't always inside jokes or nicknames, but can be something that is done rather than said. Sometimes, actions speak louder than words.

The Kissing Hand

By Robin Hobenstern

1. **SUPPLIES:** Walls patterned: Great Room Floral, Dark Chocolate Stripe; Foundations: Spruce; I.D. Tags: Fawn; Molding: Olive; Nails: Antique Flower; Address Stickers: Sand; Frame: Fawn; Other: Ribbon by May Arts; PSX stamps; Script stamp: Inkadoo; Nick Bantock Ink: Brown; Metallic Rub-ons; Date Stamp from Office Depot; Charm: "You and Me" from www.twopeasinabucket.com; Font: Marita Medium

2. **TIP:** Use metallic rubons on the embossed frames to give them a different look. Or, use the Foundations if you want a good heavy cardstock and aren't quite sure what to do with the pre-set pattern.

3. **MAKE IT MEANINGFUL:** My daughter Claire has had the book "The Kissing Hand" read to her several times at daycare, as did her brother Jacob. He outgrew the practice shortly after starting kindergarten, but now that Claire is in preschool, we have started reading "The Kissing Hand" with her. Whenever I drop her off at school, or when I leave for work, we give each other a kiss on the palm of the hand. When we are lonely, we can touch our hand to our cheek and get a warm kiss from the other person - it is our own "secret language".

Aliases

By Melanie Baur

1. **SUPPLIES:** Patterned Paper: Rec Room: Scarlet Posie, Scarlet & Butter Stripes; Cardstock: Dark Fawn, Light Butter; Nails: Fawn; I.D. Tags: Scarlet; Address Stickers: Butter; Molding: Fawn, Scarlet; Frames: Rec Room; Other: Pen by Zig Millennium; Alphabet stamps by Hero Arts and PSX; Ink by Nick Bantock; Font: Two Peas in a Bucket– 2Ps Evergreen

2. **TIP:** To convey some of the aliases that Thomas has, I stamped them on the molding that I threaded through the frame. This allowed me to include them without cluttering my journaling with additional information.

3. **MAKE IT MEANINGFUL:** Thomas has so many nicknames! They change by the week, then are forgotten. By documenting some of the funny names that we call him, we'll be able to look back and remember all of the crazy phases he's gone through.

WINdsHieLd wIpeR FLIRTationS ♥

Before we were officially dating, Adam and I would flirt like crazy. He was a bartender and worked very late hours. At the time, I worked in a daycare center and had to be at work by 7:00am. It was very difficult for me to wait for him until he got off of work because he usually wasn't done until close to 3:00am. So, I would go to his bar and usually hang out until midnight or shortly after. When I left, I always went to the parking lot and put the windshield wipers up on his car. What began as an annoying little flirtatious gesture became a way of telling him that I was thinking of him, and that I was hoping that he was thinking of me when he got off work. This little gesture seemed to carry on for quite some time and became our secret way of telling one another we are thinking of each other. Now that we are married, there is rarely a time I will come across Adam's car when I am not with him. I often think of driving to his work during the day and just putting up his windshield wipers so he'll know I still am crazy about him after all of these years, and I still do enjoy flirting with him. So, if you ever should see *my* windshield wipers up, please leave them that way...it's a message from my husband.

Windshield Wiper Flirtations

by Candi Gershon

1. **SUPPLIES:** Patterned Paper: Sitting Room: Sitting Stripe, Sitting Weave, Small Sitting Plaid; Cardstock: Light Fawn; Tacks: Denim Flower; Rivets: Denim; Address Stickers: Denim; Fonts: P22 Garamouche

2. **TIP:** Sanding just the edges of your journaling blocks and photo mats will add texture and contrast.

3. **MAKE IT MEANINGFUL:** My husband and I have a silly way we show one another that we are thinking of them. The tradition of putting up the windshield wipers on one another's cars started way back before we even started dating and were in the earliest stages of our flirtation.

Our Lines

by Ann-Marie Weis

1. **SUPPLIES:** Patterned Paper: Great Room: Scarlet Weave, Gallery: Gallery Skinny Stripe, Chocolate Gallery Dot; Cardstock: Dark Burgundy, Light Taupe; Tacks: White Round; Address Stickers: Black Chippy Circles; Other: transparency film by Office Max; Fonts: Copperplate Gothic, Bodoni, Mom's Typewriter, Forte, Baskerville Old Face, Goudy Stout, Drew, downloaded from the Internet

2. **TIP:** I used torn and cut strips of Gallery and Great Room paper to emphasize each line from our favorite movie quotations. The lines were printed on a transparency and fastened with two tacks.

3. **MAKE IT MEANINGFUL:** The lines on this page are expressions my husband and I use everyday. They have practically become a secret language for us, and we often find ourselves explaining to others what we refer to with these lines. I wanted to document this for ourselves as much as for our children. Who knows if we'll still use these lines in 10 or 20 years, but right now they are very much a part of our relationship, and I wanted to make sure that I will always remember them.

the DESIGNERS

Ruth DeFauw

It all starts with regret. I never want to regret not sharing my feelings with my family and friends because it was too hard to say it out-loud. I want to have this assurance that my love is recorded and documented for my family. That perfect assurance is my scrapbooking. And I know that this is true.

Jlyne Hanback

Scrapbooking is very important to me because every moment that I live with my family and friends is a special moment. I want to document every precious moment that I can, to ensure that future generations will see what a blessed life I lead. Scrapbooking for me is also a very important method of self-expression. It allows me to convey my thoughts and feelings through artwork. My children will be able to look at my scrapbook pages and know exactly how I felt at each stage in their lives through my meaningful journaling and detailed remembrances.

Heather Preckel

I love the fact that I am creating a legacy for my family and recording the deepest parts of my heart to them. They will know exactly how I felt about them and never question the love I put into my pages and the love that overflowed from this fabulous hobby. I love pushing my creative limits and creating masterpieces to share with friends and family. I love having a outlet to let my talents shine. Scrapbooking has opened up doors for me I would have never found otherwise, relationships I wouldn't have the privledge of having, and opportunites beyond my dreams!

Kari Barrera

I love the outlet that scrapbooking gives me. Not only does it combine two of my favorite things, creativity and talking about my family, but it really allows me to feel like I am creating a gift for my future family. I love being able to sit down and document my thoughts about the moments I've captured on film. I feel like I am having a conversation with them about what a fantastic honor it has been to be a part of their lives and to witness all the moments of their childhoods.

Jayla Campbell

The one thing that keeps me going, that drives me to continue to scrapbook, is merely to preserve my family's history. I have recently come across a journal that my grandfather kept when he was in his early twenties. I was quickly brought back to the reason why I scrapbook. I realized that scrapbooking isn't about how beautiful you can make paper look in a book. It is capturing a feeling, a memory. I hope that someday my children and my children's children will appreciate the memories I have spent many hours recording. That will be my reward!

Kristi Baumgarten

It is so important to me to document not only our family pictures, but also our memories and stories. I love to scrap about the daily things in our lives, such as conversations I have with my children that I never want to forget. I know that if I didn't scrap about them I would forget all of the small details. Sometimes I wish I could just freeze my children in the ages they are right now, but since that isn't possible, scrapbooking their lives is the next best thing! I feel very fortunate that I have found such a fun, creative way to record our memories.

CQNV ERSA TLON

WITH GAVIN. At two and a half you're quite the talker. And while a lot of it is still baby jibberish, that doesn't mean our conversations are anything less. A typical conversation for us could be -- ME: Gavin, do you want to take a nap? YOU: No. ME: Okay, do you want to play cars? YOU: No. ME: Okay, would you rather play your Jump-Start CD? YOU: No. ME: Okay, how about if I take some pictures of you? YOU: No. ME: Are you going to answer no to all of my questions? YOU: No. -- As you can plainly see, "no" is one of your favorite words and a common occurrence in our conversations. Of course, you do say other words too, but our "no" conversations always amuse me (and I know you get a kick out of it too!). I know it won't be long before we'll be conversing about world news, but for now I'm just enjoying our toddler "conversations". I know the time will pass all too quickly.

CONVERSATIONS

CONVERSATIONS

The most important things in life or significant moments in history include, if not start out with, a conversation. How fantastic would it be to have been able to be present for some of those life-changing conversations?

A unique and compelling way to journal is to document conversations in your life that changed the way you looked at something, that resulted in an important decision being made, or that just made you laugh.

Think about times in your life when you came to a place where you had to make an important choice…think about who helped you make those choices and what was said in the conversations leading-up to those choices.

Remember back to times in your life when you had an "a-ha" experience, or an experience that changed the way that you looked at or understood the world. Was a conversation part of that experience?

Think about funny things that your children or friends have said, and have maybe even turned into 'inside jokes". Write down how that conversation went, and where it's gone from there.

Try to recall in as much detail the conversations that you had with your parents, when they were teaching you about values, or work or their dreams for you.

Recall the words exchanged when you decided what college to go to, to get married, or to have children…whether the conversation was with your spouse, your best friend, your counselor, or someone you met at the airport. If you can't remember the specifics, have a conversation about it with someone now, and write down what was said during that conversation.

For the first 10 years of our marriage, my husband and I had the same ongoing conversation when we drove past a certain charming old farmhouse. That conversation is now so meaningful to me, because it resulted in the decision to sacrifice other things in our life, to buy that house and to never look back. I just love thinking about all the years we spent dreaming about living in a 'house like that' someday, and I want to have my grandchildren reading about that conversation while they are sitting in that very house visiting Grandpa and Grandma Ross.

The terrific part of journaling this way is that it is so natural. It's usually so much easier to talk through something with someone than it is to work out the words on paper. It's also really interesting for others to read.

Sweet Compassion

by Jennifer Bourgeault

1. **SUPPLIES:** Patterned Paper: Sun Room: Sun Room Stripe, Rec Room: Denim Stars; Cardstock: Dark Burgundy and Butter; Molding: Scarlet; I.D. Tags: Denim; Tacks: Tangerine; Buttons: Sun Room (Junkitz); Other: Blue and Orange Inks by VersaColor (Tsukineko); Letter Stamps: Colorbok, DMC Floss; Font: President (downloaded from www.scrapvillage.com); Stenciling Template: Wordsworth

2. **TIP:** I threaded blue string through the holes in the molding. I also printed captions on vellum and adhered them to rectangle Chatterbox I.D. Tags with the tacks.

3. **MAKE IT MEANINGFUL:** I am so used to doing things for my son, Connor, and always love doing so, but I was caught by surprise when this particular day he was the one comforting me. I was so touched by our "conversation", I wanted to make a special page to document it.

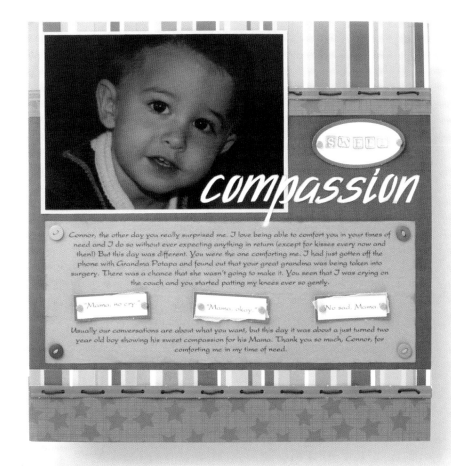

Thoughts on being a Mommy

by Heather Preckel

1. **SUPPLIES:** Patterned Paper: Powder Room: Tangerine Posie; Sunroom: Stripe and Sunny Plaid; Cardstock: Dark Tangerine; Love Tiles: Sun Room; Scrapbook Molding: Tangerine and Denim; Scrapbook Nails: Tangerine and Denim Round; Address Stickers: Tangerine and Denim; Other: Ribbon-Offray; Tags-Avery; Font: P22 Garamouche downloaded from the Internet

2. **TIP:** Use different colors of scrapbook letters for a title that stands out. Use molding in different lengths of strips for accents. Fold down corner of double sided paper to show both sides.

3. **MAKE IT MEANINGFUL:** The instant I got this picture back I knew that I wanted to do some kind of page about being a mommy. Just looking at my little girl look at her baby that way was so special. I felt almost fulfilled as a mom knowing I was passing down nurturing qualities to my little girl that she would treat her babies in this way.

I Said, He Said

by Tarri Botwinski

1. **SUPPLIES:** Walls Patterned: Billiard Room: Billiard Pinstripe, Billiard Stripe, Rec Room: Rec Blocks, Cardstock: Dark Burgundy, Light Fawn, Dark Olive, Dark Denim, Nails: Burgundy, Denim, Molding: Burgundy, Denim, Frames: Billiard Room, Other: Jute, PSX Antiques Alphabet Stamps, Ink: Close To My Heart, Font: Harting- Internet

2. **TIP:** I laced jute through the molding. I used straight lines and angles to give the layout a more "masculine" feel.

3. **MAKE IT MEANINGFUL:** My son, Riley, is eight years old and won't believe in things like Santa for much longer. I love our conversations, and I wanted to document this one so I would always remember there was a time that he still believed.

Loyal Companion

by Beth Hooper

1. **SUPPLIES:** Patterned Paper: Cabin: Olive Daisy, Sitting Room: Sitting flowers; Cardstock: Dark Denim; Frame: Tan; Love Tiles: Memories; Address Stickers: Black Chippy; Other: Vellum: Bazzill; Alpha Stamps: Antique Alpha by PSX; Stamping Ink: Memories (black), Nick Bantock (Van Dyke Brown); Dymo Label Maker; Black and white Gingham Ribbon by Offray; Letter Stickers: Wordsworth

2. **TIP:** Use a manilla envelope as a template and create an envelope out of Chatterbox paper.

3. **MAKE IT MEANINGFUL:** Meredith has always been a very curious child. Since being able to talk, she has been full of questions. One day, our conversation was regarding the loss of our pet, Rocky. Thru this conversation, I realized that she truly would enjoy having a new pet to love. It also opened my eyes to what a compassionate and caring person she is growing into.

Chatterbox

by Kristi Baumgarten

1. **SUPPLIES:** Patterned paper: Great Room: Scarlet Bloom, Chocolate Bloom, Cardstock: Dark Olive, Light Sand; Address Stickers: Black Chippy; Tacks: Scarlet; Other: drywall mesh; button, twine, ribbon, tag; Fonts: Dymo, Elronet Monospace

2. **TIP:** Use fonts to create Dymo-like labels.

3. **MAKE IT MEANINGFUL:** I like to journal about my children's quirks and personalities. Chloe is such a little chatterbox, and I don't ever want her to forget it...she sure won't let me!

Christmas Love

by Kristi Baumgarten

1. **SUPPLIES:** Patterned Paper: Reading Room: Holiday Plaid; Cardstock: Dark Olive, Other: ribbon, buttons; Dymo label maker, transparency; Fonts: 2Ps Jack Frost, Arial

2. **TIP:** Print title out on a transparency

3. **MAKE IT MEANINGFUL:** I don't ever want to forget the conversations that I overhear between my children. Journaling about them on my scrapbook pages is the perfect way to record them.

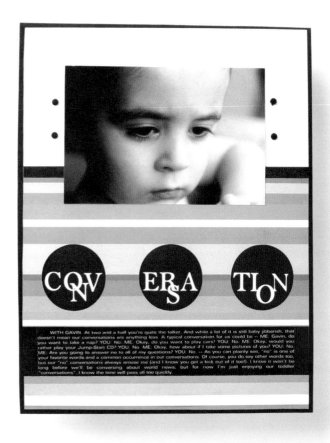

A Conversation with Gavin

by Desiree McClellen

1. **SUPPLIES:** Patterned Paper: Den Room: Big Den Stripe; Address Stickers: White; Tacks: Black Round; Font: Zurich

2. **TIP:** For the title, I cut circles in the patterned paper and placed the letter stickers on the black cardstock underneath.

3. **MAKE IT MEANINGFUL:** At two and a half, my sons favorite word is undoubtedly "no". It finds its way into all of our conversations, and is a common answer to most of my questions! I wanted to scrap a typical "no" conversation between us to remind us of these memorable times.

Boy Cheese Sandwich

by Christy Tomlinson

1. **SUPPLIES:** Patterned Paper: Cottage: Sky Cottage, Sitting Room: Pebble Stripe, Taupe Quilt, Sun Room: Sun Room Weave; Cardstock: Taupe (Bazzill); Letter Stencil: Chocolate; Rub-ons: Chippy Brown; Font: Chatterbox Rust and Lablemaker; Other: Staples; Ribbon: Making Memories and May Arts; Corrugated Paper

2. **TIP:** Use staples to adhere pictures, titles, and journaling. I also backed my letter stencils with paper and put ink on them. I used my sewing machine to add interest as well.

3. **MAKE IT MEANINGFUL:** My son Preston is 100% ALL boy. Everything he does has to be boyish. He loves getting dirty and doing "boyish" things. It was no surprise when my husband relayed this story to me about the grilled-cheese sandwich:

One day while cooking lunch, he asked Allie and Preston, "What do you want for lunch?"

Allie answered, "I want a grilled-cheese sandwich."

Then Ben asked, "Preston, do you want a grilled-cheese sandwich too?"

Preston scrunched up his face in disgust and replied, "I don't want a GIRL-cheese sandwich, I want a BOY-cheese sandwich!"

Kids are just too funny!

Conversations with Kyle

by Candi Gershon

1. **SUPPLIES:** Patterned Paper: Billiard Room: Billiard Stripes, Billiard Circles, Billiard Pinstripes, Billiard Plaid, Billiard Table; Cardstock: Light Denim Solid; Tacks: Denim Round & Square, Antique Bronze Round, Scarlet Star & Flower; Nails: Denim; Windows; Address Stickers: Scarlet & Scarlet Chippy; Love Tiles: Billiard; Other: pressed flower; Stamps: PSX, Making Memories letter stamps

2. **TIP:** Use Windows to protect fragile items such as a pressed flower.

3. **MAKE IT MEANINGFUL:** My son is quite the talker for someone who is under the age of three. I spent a period of a couple of weeks writing down the little conversations we have and I recorded them in this mini album. I divided each conversation by topic and titled each page to correspond with an aspect of his personality.

Believe

by Erica Hernandez

1. **SUPPLIES:** Patterned Paper: Cabin: Burgundy Daisy; Cardstock: Fawn; Address Stickers: Scarlet; Rivets: Antique Gold; Tag: Round Scarlet; Waxy Flax: Scrapworks; Stencil: unknown

2. **TIP:** I used Chatterbox cardstock to create the frame for the picture. Just miter the corners and lightly sand the edges of the cardstock to distress.

3. **MAKE IT MEANINGFUL:** My sister has always had a unique perspective on things. I used this layout to document a conversation that shows her personality very well.

scrapbooking

E-MAILS

may '04

jessi STRINGERS

attie

It's the little things in life that make your day complete. The day I received this email from my friend Christy, happened to be one of those days.

Two weeks earlier, I had spent five days in the Tomlinson home, hanging out with my friends Christy and Ruth. Never did I consider that I was going to make yet another good friend while I was up there, especially with a four year old. Meaning, kids always seem to love me, but c'mon, I was only there for five days. I'm not family, and I live 369 miles away.

But as fate would have it, I'm 24 years older than my new best friend, doesn't make any difference...

scrapbooking E-MAILS

If you are avid e-mailer, you have probably recapped your daily events many times over through e-mails to family, friends and coworkers. Have you thought about how much of it could be used as journaling? If nothing else, it is excellent factual information to put into your personal journal.

You likely have a lot of meaningful correspondence in e-mails sent back and forth between you and the important people in your life. The brilliant fact about your e-mails is you have a copy of what you sent out, as well as what was sent back to you...and you can actually read the conversation between two people.

I catch up with old friends throughout the year through e-mails. As I was doing a yearly recap for a friend a few years ago, I realized how much information I was gathering I hadn't even written in my journal. I simply copied my typed-out, summarized year and pasted it into my journal. I learned I could benefit from all of the e-mails I send and receive by copying and pasting the information, and not even having to retype it. These bits of journaling can be used in your scrapbooks, or kept as memorabilia.

As you are writing e-mails to others, think about how you can make the most of what you are writing. Can the words you are typing be used to make a great memory album layout? Can they be kept as a personal history? Can you add more personal feelings after you send the e-mail and then put it into your journal?

You can print out the actual e-mail as it exists, with the date, time sent, email addresses, etc., or you can take all of the technicality out of it, change the fonts and ink colors, and make it more decorative before you print it out.

Using e-mails as journaling works as a time saver and also takes the inhibition out of journaling for your scrapbooks. Because you are 'talking' to someone else through e-mail, your personality is reflected, which is sometimes hard to do when you are simply journaling for your albums.

Read through your e-mails and think about what the words might mean to you in 10 years, or in 50 years. Think of them as handwritten letters, because in this day and age, they are the equivalent of what handwritten letters were 25 years ago. You probably would never throw away a meaningful letter, so think it through before you hit the delete button in your e-mail program.

Jessi Stringers

by Jessi Stringham

1. **SUPPLIES:** Patterned Paper: Gallery: Chocolate Gallery Swirl, Light Chocolate Open Dot, Chocolate Pinstripe, Cabin: Olive Daisy; Cardstock: Dark Chocolate; Address Stickers: White and Olive; Buttons: Chatterbox by Junkitz (Cabin); Other: Ribbon: MayArts; Fonts: Century Gothic; Ink: Ranger Industries– Distress Ink

2. **TIP:** Instead of using all of the same color of Address Stickers, change it up! Use two different colors to add some fun to the title. If you want to use a button and string envelope on your layout, and you want it to coordinate with your layout, use your favorite Chatterbox patterned paper and create your own! If there isn't enough room on your page to display the envelope, create a secret pocket by cutting with an Xacto knife along the stripe in the patterned paper, and slide it in and tie it shut with decorative ribbon.

3. **MAKE IT MEANINGFUL:** The day I received this e-mail, I was having "one of those days" where you think to yourself, "Do I really make a difference in others' lives?" Then I received this e-mail, and I realized that even in the simplest of ways, I touch people's lives every day, regardless if they tell me or not. Because I was fortunate to receive this e-mail, I decided to print it off and document how darling Allie was for saying this stuff to her mom about me.

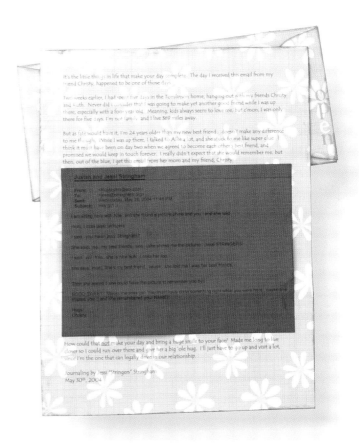

Allison

by Jessi Stringham

1. **SUPPLIES:** Patterned Paper: Great Room: Great Little Stripe, Butter & Olive Stripe, Great Room Floral; Cardstock: Dark Scarlet, Dark Olive, Dark Chocolate, Light Olive; Rub-ons: Friendship; Rivets: Antique Bronze; Other: Ribbon: MayArts; Making Memories washer word and date stamp; Fonts: Century Gothic; Ink: Ranger Industries– Distress Ink

2. **TIP:** I created a small pocket to hold my journaling and the e-mail from Allison by sewing directly onto my layout. This allowed me to fit another picture on the layout of Allison. I used the Rivets as bullet points to highlight several words that describe Allison's personality using the Chatterbox Rub-ons from the Friendship package.

3. **MAKE IT MEANINGFUL:** I thought it would be neat to use several words from the Friendship package of the new Chatterbox Rub-ons to summarize my journaling in the sewn pocket. So, if people didn't want to read my journaling, they would get the general idea of what I was conveying on the layout. I kept this e-mail from Allison because it was so sweet and reminded me of how lucky I am to have her as a friend. I love surrounding myself with positive people such as herself. I feel it's important to document friendships because 50 years down the road, you may forget!

Happy 35th Birthday

by Ruth De Fauw

1. **SUPPLIES:** Patterned Paper: Billiard Table, Billiard Stripe; Cardstock: Dark Scarlet; Frames: Rec Room; Address Stickers: Black; Other: Embroidery Floss: Anchor; Font: Pharmacy from www.haroldsfonts.com; Paper clips: Zig Writer by EK Sucess; White Cardstock (unknown)

2. **TIP:** Turn your patterned paper stripes into makeshift ribbon and thread them through frames for a buckle effect.

3. **MAKE IT MEANINGFUL:** I have many amazing friends that live far away and I speak to them daily via the Internet. When my birthday passed this year, I received so many amazing e-mail messages and e-cards that I wanted to save them. I printed them off in a 4 x 6 format to make them easier to scrap.

Uncle Chris

by Robyn Werlich

1. **SUPPLIES:** Patterned Paper: Sitting Flowers; Cardstock: Light Spruce, Dark Sand; I.D. Tags: Spruce; Molding: Spruce; Tacks: Antique Gold Flowers; Other: Van Dyke Brown Ink by Ranger; Ribbon by Stampin' Up!; Marker from Stampin' Up!; Staples

2. **TIP:** Cut a straight line with your Xacto knife to provide a fun slit to slide your photo and journaling under.

3. **MAKE IT MEANINGFUL:** When Madisyn's uncle left to serve a mission in Russia, it was sad to realize that he would be missing two years of her life. To help us, and my daughter Madisyn, know what he is doing and why it is so important, I plan to create a monthly layout, with direct journaling from his weekly e-mails to us. Hopefully it will be a wonderful memory in the years to come.

Friends

by Christy Tomlinson

1. **SUPPLIES:** Patterned Paper: Scarlet & Butter Stripe, Great Room Plaid; Cardsock: Light Olive, Dark Scarlet; Frames: Gallery Khaki; Other: Ink: Tim Holtz Distressed Ink by Ranger- Vintage Photo; Buttons; Ribbon: Offray

2. **TIP:** I created a pocket on my page using my sewing machine and paper. Then I backed my cardstock with another piece of cardstock to keep it sturdy. I hand-wrote my journaling to give it a more personal effect.

3. **MAKE IT MEANINGFUL:** Mel and I hit it off the first time we actually had a sit down conversation. I was visiting her house while on vacation. After I got home, the only way we communicated was through e-mail. Our e-mails were always so emotional and full of thoughts about life, love, family, and work. We've became such close friends in such a short amount of time through our e-mail conversations. I can truly say I am so grateful I saved all those e-mails. She is one of my best friends, and her insight and encouragement about life will be something I will always remember.

Insight

by Alison Chabe

1. **SUPPLIES:** Walls Patterned: Gallery: Gallery Stripe, Light Chocolate Open Dot; Cardstock: Light Taupe, Black (Bazzill); Tacks: Antique Gold Round and Flower; I.D. Tags: Black; Molding: Black.; Address Stickers: Black & Black Chippy Circles; Other: Copper Ink by Color Box

2. **TIP:** Use tacks as bullets when listing thoughts or phrases.

3. **MAKE IT MEANINGFUL:** Because my husband was gone a lot more than he had been in the past, I was having a little trouble adjusting to his new work hours. I hadn't said anything to him about it, because I knew it was just as hard on him. Then one night, he sent me this e-mail, and it really put everything back into perspective. Instead of journaling about the circumstance surrounding his e-mail, I chose to journal the thoughts I had when I received it.

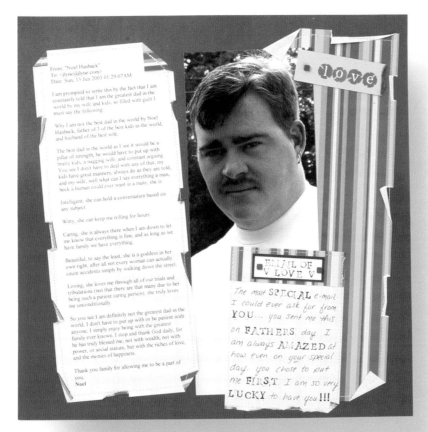

E-mail of Love

by Jlyne Hanback

1. **SUPPLIES:** Patterned Paper: Rec Room: Scarlet & Butter Stripes; Cardstock: Dark Burgundy; Tacks: Scarlet Square; Adress Stickers: Burgundy Chippy Circles; I.D. Tags: Burgundy; Other: Machine Stitching, Printers Type Letter Stamps by Hero Arts, Black Staz-On Inkpad by Tsukineko

2. **TIP:** Mix stamped letters with your own handwriting for an interesting journaling effect.

3. **MAKE IT MEANINGFUL:** Last Father's Day, my husband sent me the most heartfelt e-mail that I will always treasure. To preserve it, I printed it out on patterned paper and incorporated it into my layout.

the DESIGNERS

Vanessa Reyes

Through all of my years, and all of my memories, I have enjoyed the treasures I have created through scrapbooking the most. I say this because these are the most vivid and emotional parts of my memories. To be able to capture a feeling or a celebration of life in a timeless way is my most prized possession. I am so thankful that I can not only create a lifetime of saved memories for my family, but I can also share these priceless moments with new friends and new additions for years to come.

Robyn Weirlich

In 2002, I started scrapbooking as a way to document my thoughts and feelings for my daughter. Since then, it has grown into an intensely important passion in my life. It is my creative outlet, my emotional release. I've realized I look at life completely different. I absorb those special moments with my sweet children and husband, then I grab the camera and capture them on film. I keep journals of our conversations, feelings, and moments I don't want to ever forget. I am preserving our memories now so we will have them to cherish for a lifetime.

Melanie Bauer

I love the fact that years from now when my family consists of more than me, my husband the medical student, and my crazy cat, that my children and future generations will be able to look back on layouts in my albums and know "the me" that I am today. "The me" that they weren't there to experience first hand, but "the me" they can look back on through time of joy and times of crisis. "The me" before – that's why I treasure scrapbooking so much.

Other Contributing Designers:

Alison Chabe
Heather Melzer
Carolyn Peeler
Erica Hernandez
Robin Hohenstern
Rachel Ludwig
Amy Yingling

Mellette Berezoski

Ever since I was a little girl, I have kept journals of my thoughts, hopes, and feelings. I hope that the memories preserved in my scrapbooks will lend some insight into who I was and what was important to me. Years from now I want to be able to sit on the front porch with my husband, laughing and crying with each turn of the page, remembering the way our lives were at that moment. I love that through scrapbooking, thoughts, feelings, morals, values, and memories can live on over generations. It is such an important and cherished part of my life.

letters from OTHERS

letters from OTHERS

Letters are less and less common in this day of technology, so if you're lucky enough to have a handwritten or typed out letter, or collection of correspondence through letters, it's definitely worth scrapbooking.

A few times in my marriage, my husband has written me notes or something really special inside of a card. For my husband, this is a great leap, as he prefers to show his love through daily acts and words. Those letters and cards are like prized diamonds to me. I can write all about the romantic and selfless acts that he commits in my honor, but to actually have notes and letters from him means everything to me, as if I can hear his voice over and over again as many times as I wish to...that is the beauty of the written word.

Children are legendary for writing beautiful notes and letters. Correspondence from children is certainly worthy of painstaking archiving. I think I have every letter from each of my 5 children, plus every picture drawn. Their kindergarten handwriting tells a story all it's own, as much as their pre-teen hearts dotting the 'i's'.

I also have priceless, life changing letters between my older sister and I that are in chronological order, as if we were having a written conversation back and forth over the course of many years. Because they are such an important part of my life, I plan to give these letters a home in their own album. If you have had that kind of consistent correspondence from long-distance relationships, times away, or pen pals, you can create an entire album of just letters.

Using a letter for your journaling is as easy as delegating the journaling out. Unless there are particular feelings you want to document in relation to the letter, you can use the letters to tell the whole story, and forego any writing on your part.

If you are reluctant to use your original letters in your scrapbooks, simply make color copies of them. (It's a good idea to make copies of irreplaceable memorabilia in any case.) This is especially important if you are using letters that are important to you, but don't belong to you, such as age-old teenage love letters between your parents that your mother has under her bed. Let her know you'll return them safely as soon as you make copies.

You can mount a letter on a scrapbook page, or you can create an envelope or pocket for it to slip into, still folded, on the page. If you have the original postmarked envelope, that's a lovely memento to include, as well.

Pull the letters out of the shoeboxes and realize their potential! Ask your parents and grandparents if they have any letters they would be willing to let you get your hands on. If you wrote letters home while in college or away from home, ask your mother for copies of them, you'll love reading what you wrote, and so will your children. Keep every letter you receive from this moment on, you will be so glad you did!

Sister

by Candi Gershon

1. **SUPPLIES:** Patterned Paper: Parlor: Parlor Posies, Parlor Stripes, Parlor Plaid, Parlor Posies Vellum, Sun Room: Sunny Flowers; Cardstock: Light Spruce; Tacks: Violet Flowers; I.D. Tags: Spruce; Address Stickers: Violet; Buttons: Chatterbox by Junkitz (Parlor Room); Other: Ribbon by Ofray, Vellum Envelope, Ink by ColorBox, Ancient Page; Fonts: LD Letterpress, 2Peas Hot Chocolate, 2Peas Wedding Day

2. **TIP:** Make an interesting photo mat by rolling the double sided paper to reveal the pattern/color on the backside.

3. **MAKE IT MEANINGFUL:** When I turned 29, my sister sent me a card with a heartfelt letter inside telling me how much I mean to her, and how the miles that separate us have only brought us closer emotionally. I scanned in her letter and printed it on coordinating paper. I also included the postmark from the envelope.

My Wonderful Friend, Julie

by Jessi Stringham

1. **SUPPLIES:** Patterned Paper: Sun Room: Pool Tiles (reverse side), Sunny Flowers, Sun Room Weave, Gallery: Dark Gallery Swirl, Rec Room: Scarlet Dots; Cardstock: Dark Scarlet Solid; Mailboxes: Sun; Rub-Ons: Friendship; Tacks: Scarlet; Other: Ribbon: MayArts (polka dots), Silk Ribbon (unknown); Making Memories date stamp; Fonts: Emmascript (congratulations) and Century Gothic for rest of text; Ink: Ranger Industries– Distress Ink

2. **TIP:** I mixed a couple different Chatterbox rooms together for a completely different look. The new Chatterbox Mailboxes are so simple to just add directly onto a layout to hold any sort of memorabilia.

3. **MAKE IT MEANINGFUL:** I've had this card since 1999, because that is the year Julie and I graduated from college. It was important for me to capture this moment on a layout, because she was such a huge influence in my life at that time. She continues to be one of my dearest friends to this day.

Carmel Apple

by Carrie Utley

1. **SUPPLIES:** Patterned Paper: Powder Stripe; Cardstock: Dark Tangerine; Windows: Round; Other: Ribbon: Offray; Jewelry Rings: Darice; Daisy Punch: Family Treasures; Date Stamp: Staples; Ink: Tsukineko, Inc.

2. **TIP:** Create more journaling space by adding layers. I attached an extra vellum page to the layout which gave me more room to include both my journaling and my daughter's. You can also include a sample of your own handwriting by including important details on strips of paper or other borders on your page. I wrote the event on a piece of ribbon which I attached to the spine of the layout. To add more dimension, create "ruffled" edges by tearing and rolling the edges of a border strip and then layering another torn and rolled border strip over the top.

3. **MAKE IT MEANINGFUL:** Children can add very vivid details to memory journaling. Because children absorb everything about their enviroment all the time, they tend to be very open and honest with their journaling. Their senses are open to sights, sounds, tastes, and smells. My daughter has a very special relationship with her grandmother, and I wanted her viewpoint of some photos that were taken at a carnival I wasn't able to attend with them. Instead of interviewing her, I turned over the pen and paper and let her do it all herself. I was surprised at how much she had to say and how quickly she jotted everything down. I included the journal page written in her own handwriting and added my own emotions about the photos as hidden journaling on the inside pages.

Love Letters

by Jayla Campbell

1. **SUPPLIES:** Patterned Paper: Scarlet and Butter Stripe, Scarlet Poise Vellum; Cardstock: Dark Scarlet; Tacks: Antique Bronze Round; Other: Envelope with cut out center and clear vellum, Ribbon, Brown Cardstock

2. **TIP:** Cut out the center of a small envelope and cover it with vellum to create a window. This allows you to still see your notes.

3. **MAKE IT MEANINGFUL:** I cherish every little note my husband has given me. They bring back so many fun memories. They have been sitting in my jewelry box until now. With them being a part of my scrapbook now, I no longer fear they will be lost or misplaced.

Becky

by Jayla Campbell

1. **SUPPLIES:** Patterned Paper: Cottage; Rosey Bouquet; Cardstock: Dark Spruce; Rivets: Spruce; Tacks: Rosey Flowers; Other: Wire, Ribbon, Love Charm

2. **TIP:** Sew a pocket on your page to keep meaningful letters in.

3. **MAKE IT MEANINGFUL:** My sister, Becky, is one of the most amazing people I know. I look up to her in so many ways. I have carried this letter with me for the last 18 years. It was satisfying to finally add this to my scrapbook. It is now something that can be shared with my children.

Homecoming

by Brooke Campbell

1. **SUPPLIES:** Patterned Paper: Cabin: Burgundy Daisy; Cardstock: Dark Scarlet; Tacks: White Round; Other: netting, black ribbon, black chalk, and CK Elegant font

2. **TIP:** Make embellishments of your own design like the flowers on this page.

3. **MAKE IT MEANINGFUL:** Grady went to Homecoming with his girlfriend, Nicole. They had a really fun time together, so I had him write a short letter to her to put with their picture.

Acceptance

by Melanie Bauer

1. **SUPPLIES:** Walls Patterned: Sitting Room: Sitting Stripe; Cardstock: Light Fawn; Tacks: Antique Bronze Square; Molding: Fawn; I.D. Tags: Fawn; Address Stickers: Fawn; Other: Ribbon by Making Memories, Label Tape by Dymo, Pen by Zig Millennium

2. **TIP:** Use strips of Scrapbook Molding and Tacks to anchor a letter or other piece of memorabilia. It's held onto the page, but can be removed to be viewed more closely.

3. **MAKE IT MEANINGFUL:** Most people have their acceptance letter from college, but what's the story behind the letter? I used it as a starting point to convey what I was doing when I received the letter, as well as a conversation with my mom during the application process.

Love Letters

by Christy Tomlinson

1. **SUPPLIES:** Patterned Paper: Great Room: Scarlet Bloom, Great Room Floral, Butter & Olive Stripe; Cardstock: Dark Chocolate; Mailboxes: Great Room; Tags: Great Room; Rubons: Heber Brown; Other: Ink: Tim Holtz Distressed Ink by Ranger-Vintage Photo; Flower: Prima; Buttons, Ribbon, Date Stamp & Small Cream Tag: Making Memories; Font: Emma Script- downloaded from the Internet

2. **TIP:** I love layering papers, and I used this to technique throughout the entire layout. I not only layered the patterned paper, but the photo, tags, and mailbox as well.

3. **MAKE IT MEANINGFUL:** It isn't everyday you receive a "love letter" from more than one person. I guess I must be lucky, because on this particular day, I received four. My children are constantly reminding me of how much I truly am blessed to have them in my life. I love the little things they do that make all the difference.

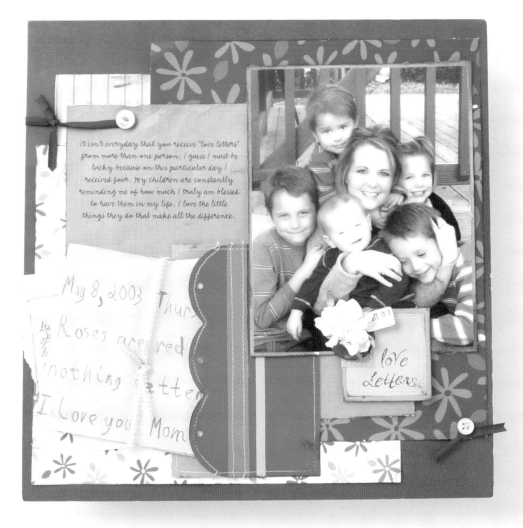

journaling PROMPTS

Use these prompts to create themed pages or albums.

Buddies
How we are alike
How we are different
Showing our muscles
Our funniest faces
What we like to do together
Our favorite way to get into trouble

My Grandparents
Grandma
Grandpa
What they always tell me
What I learned from their example
The role they have played in my life
How I want to make them proud
The best advice they have given me
The ways that I take after them

Our Family
Our favorite activity together
Our favorite place
What we are known for
Our family photo
Our favorite meal
Words to describe us

My Goals
For my mind
For my relationships
For my career
For my body
To help others
For my spirit

Our Little Boy
How we chose his name
His favorite things
His personality
How he has changed our life
The fits he throws
The funny things he does
What we want for him
His smile

What I Love About You
Your sense of humor
Your smile
Your company
Pretty much everything
Your laugh
Your quirks
Your good intentions
Your hugs

My Father
My best memory of him
The best lesson I've learned from him
What he always says
Ways that I take after him
Words to describe him
How he has affected my life

All About My Son
What I love most about him
What I have learned from him
What makes me proud of him
What he does best
How I would describe him
How he has changed my life

Best Friends
How we met
Our favorite things
Where we hang out together
What we mean to each other
How we are alike
How we are different

Our Little Girl
How we chose her name
Her favorite things
Her personality
How she has changed our life
The fits she throws
The funny things she does
What we want for her
Her smile

One Wild Time
What we still talk about
Who was there
How we planned it
What I'll never forget about this
The best part
What's going on in this picture
The craziest part
The funniest memory

Me & the Girls
Inside jokes
Our best memories
How to describe us
What's fun about us
What we love to do
Our favorite hang-out

My Sister
What I love most about her
Ways that I admire her
The best lesson I've learned from her
My best memory with her
Words to describe her
What makes me proud of her

Our Town
Our schools
Our church
Our population sign
Main street
Our stores
Our post office

Christmas at Our House
Our traditional feast
Our most fun tradition
How we celebrate
Our favorite part of the season
How we decorate our home
Who we spend the holiday with
The best gifts
What Christmas means to us

Our Home
The back
The front
The rooms
The story of our home
What we love most
What we would change

A Day in My Life

How I end the day
How I start the day
Where I go
My favorite part of the day
Who I love to see
What I wish I could change
What I live for
What I have to do

My Brother

Words to describe him
What he has taught me
Our best memories together
What he means to me
How we are alike
How we are different

My Daughter

What makes me proud of her
What she does best
What I love most about her
How I would describe her
What I have learned from her
How she has changed my life

We Love U.S.A.

Our flag
Why we are proud of our country
Our American heritage
What we love about America
What we want for our country
How we show our patriotism

Your Friendship

You are
How you've changed my life
What I'll always remember about you
What I've learned from you
What I like most about you
My favorite memory with you

Why You're My Hero

Your integrity
Your accomplishments
Your dedication
Your attitude
Your ambition
Your generosity

Our Trip

What we did
The map
Where we went
Who we went with
What we ate
How we got there
The best part
The worst part

My Pet

Funny things
Memories
What my pet means to me
Sweet things
Our history together
My pet's favorite things

School Days

My friends
Teachers
Good parts
Not-so-good parts
My schedule
Activities
My school stuff
Classes

My Story

Me then
Me now
The steps I took
What I experienced
How I've changed
What I learned
The worst part
The best part

Thank You

For being you
For our love
For your kindness
For your support
For your company
For your friendship

The Days of Summer

A typical day
Favorite summer things
The best part
What we do
Where we go
The worst part

Family Fun

Inside jokes
All together
Goofin' around
Things we do
Funny faces
Happiness

Hangin' Out

Just us
What we do
Our favorite things
What's funny about us
Where we go
What's great about us

A Very Happy Birthday

The age
The guests
The location
How we celebrated
Fun
The food
The best part
The gifts

I Did It!

What my goal was
The feelings I have about it
The steps I took
Obstacles I overcame
How long it took
What I learned
Mistakes I made
How it changed my life

My Mother

What I love most about her
Ways that I take after her
The best lesson I've learned from her
My best memory of her
Words to describe her
What makes me proud of her

What I Wish for You

About happiness
When following your dreams
In marriage
In your career
As a parent
With friendships

Our Wedding

The cake
The guests
The bride
The groom
The wedding party
Our rings

Our Anniversary

What is unique about us
How we celebrated
What we'll always remember
How we show our love for each other
The best part
What I love about our relationship

MAKE IT MEANINGFUL.